Reversing the R

Other books by Roy Gillett

Astrological Diaries 1978-1990
A Model of Health
Zen for Modern Living
The Essence of Buddhism
Astrology and Compassion the Convenient Truth
Economy Ecology and Kindness
The Secret Language of Astrology

Reversing the Race to Global Destruction

Abandoning the Politics of Greed

Roy Gillett

***Crucial* Books**

First published in 2017 by
Crucial Books,
PO Box 1061, Camberley GU15 9PL
http://crucialbooks.co.uk/

Copyright © 2017 Roy Gillett

The author has asserted his right to be identified as
the author of this work.

All rights reserved.
No part of this publication may be reproduced or utilised in any form or by any means electronic or mechanical, including photocopying, recording or any information, storage and retrieval system now known or hereafter invented without the prior permission of the author.

A catalogue record for this book is available from the British Library.

ISBN 978-0-9956999-1-5

Printed and bound by Lightning Source

Science and technology have contributed immensely to the overall development of humankind, to our material comfort and well-being as well as to our understanding of the world we live in. But if we put too much emphasis on these endeavours, we are in danger of losing those aspects of human knowledge that contribute to the development of an honest and altruistic personality.

Science and technology cannot replace the age-old spiritual values that have been largely responsible for the true progress of world civilisation as we know it today. No one can deny the material benefits of modern life, but we are still faced with suffering, fear, and tension—perhaps more now than ever before. So it is only sensible to try to strike a balance between material development on the one side and development of spiritual values on the other. In order to bring about a great change, we need to revive and strengthen our inner values.

How to See Yourself As You Really Are
His Holiness the XlVth Dalai Lama

Contents

Preface to the Published Edition   9

Introduction - Wasted Years   11
Failed economic assumptions the root of all problems. A sounder base for capitalism. Breaking the barriers to a better world

Part One - Ways to Global Destruction

Chapter 1   The 'Global Race'- the Problem not the Solution   20
   Consequences of ignoring the Jupiter-Saturn rhythm. Believing in something better. Our times force us to change.

Chapter 2   The Problem with Economics   28
   Personal gain the essential aim. Unethical profit motivation. When profit is the enemy of an efficient economy. The nemesis of exploitative capitalism. Globalisation. The built-in failure of short-term strategies. How long can growth last? The futility of short-term economic 'sticking plasters'. The nemesis of self-deception. A better system of enterprise.

Chapter 3   The Problem with Rules and the Law   43
   The mass deceptions of 'absolute truths'. Rules and laws that divide. Rules as statements of social fashion. Rules and agreements that divide nations. Principles that could unite us. Using astrology to understand what seems to divide us. The unifying good heart that sets us free.

Chapter 4   The Problem with Today's Science & Education   56
   The benefits of modern science. The problems of modern science. How statistics can be counter-productive. The benefits and shortcomings of reductionist science. Clarifying the limits of reductionist science. The danger of relying on reductionist science. Spiritual values can contain misuse of scientific discovery. The transitory history of 'absolute truth'. Initiating the new generation in our modern world. We are educating our children in the secular faith. Education for a happy world.

Chapter 5   The Problem with Society   76
   Warrior states and empires. Contemporary societies. Cultural dictatorship by the 'meritocracy'. Consequences of not playing the game. The aristocraticisation of the proletariat. All kinds of better people can create better worlds.

Chapter 6   The Problem with the Media & Politics   86
   What's on the news? Marketing for money. Entertainment. The problem of politicians. The intelligent voter uses astro-cycles. Developing the right political attitude.

Chapter 7   The Problem with the World   98
   Ever-expanding world marketplace. No room to breathe. Defending 'our way of life'. Losing our young people. The consequences of our amoral belief system. Everyone has the solution to all their conflicts.

Part Two   Reversing the Race to Global Destruction

Chapter 8   Finding Answers to All Our Problems   110
   The rise and fall of great empires. Will consumer capitalism go the same way? The first step of a new way. Not fit for purpose. The *Golden Standard*. Not the *Golden Standard*. Implementing the *Golden Standard*. Adopting the *Golden Standard*.

Chapter 9   Applying Answers to All Our Problems   122
   Principles are rules that unify. Establishing a principle-based system of legal precedent. Using *Golden Standard* principles to improve sentencing. Building up a new kind of case law and precedent. A right relationship with the world and each other. Science and education for better lives. Restoring freedom to 'free enterprise'. Free enterprise for whom. Astro-cycles indicate growth-based capitalism's endgame. Aquarian answers?. Free enterprise for all. A political process all can embrace. Real communications.

Chapter 10 Using Astrology to Answer Problems   138
   The astrology of the Laurel and Hardy relationship. The astrology of everyone's relationship. Answering world problems. The astrology of the perpetuation of suffering. The destruction of the Jewish temple. The Middle East Mandate. The astrology of a missed opportunity. Isil - the endgame of revenge. Solving problems by looking through others' eyes. How to transform suffering into happiness. Forgiving the unforgivable - unity in international affairs. Believing such forgiveness is possible. Understanding the causes of unacceptability. Forgiving the unacceptable. Forgiveness in the twenty-first century.

Chapter 11 Open Borders – the Heart of the Answer 166
> Borders that do not protect. Removing artificial borders; *Golden Standard* second step. Celebrating and gaining from cultural differences. Doing better by having less. At last an inheritance to be thankful for. Astro-cycles and global disintegration. Astro-cycles and global regeneration. Reversing t he race to global destruction.

Chapter 12 Let's Get Real! 179
> Setbacks should encourage us to go forward. Handling setbacks that undermine ordinary life. Good heals wounds. Give goodness time to grow. Not an impossible dream. Not a dream at all. The Anthem of Love.

Notes 191

Index 195

Roy Gillett's *Astrological Quartet* 201

Acknowledgements

Thanks to Astrolabe Inc. [http://alabe.com/] for use of *Solar Fire V9* and *AstroAnalyst* software to generate astrological and price charts, Jane Struthers for her proofing and Alice Ekrek Hovanessian for the index.

The work, wisdom and achievement of numerous devoted astrologers, Buddhist friends, planetary healers and people of good will have inspired this work. Feedback from my children and grandchildren has broaden the book's academic, generational and social perception. Everyone who knows me will recognise the part they have played and will play in achieving its vision.

As always, the profoundly kind and tireless persistence of Lama Thubten Zopa Rinpoche continues to generate hope. Without Rinpoche's example and my wife Carolyn's untiring support my ability to offer these ideas would not have been possible and, in many other respects, the value of my life's endeavours would have been far less.

Preface

In 2016, Oxford Dictionaries named 'post-truth' as the Word of the Year,[1] defining its meaning as 'relating to or denoting circumstances in which objective facts are less influential in shaping public opinion than appeals to emotion and personal belief.']

Thinking like this has become so because many custodians of objective facts have been exposed as dishonest and self-serving. Opinion leaders in the business, financial, media, political, even academic, and legal worlds seem devoted to a world economy motivated by unprincipled greed. Their knowledge, legal, political and communication systems do not seem to assess objectively, but merely to justify, reinforce and trap ordinary people in harsh 'reality'.

If you cannot trust the experts, why not believe anything on the Internet or in a political campaign that feels right? Stripped by the system of the integrity of a heart felt happy life, where else can people turn, but to self-interest? In doing so, it is not emotion or personal belief that leads them astray, but the form these take.

- ❖ Negative emotional reactions to a world system devoid of fundamental integrity are the cause of many terrible things that have been happening during the writing of this book. Social collapse in parts of the Middle East leads to mass migration and terrorism. Globalisation and speculation make a few rich at the expense of everyone else.
- ❖ Positive emotional reactions seeking kindness and happiness for more and more people start us on a road beyond self-interested beliefs. These come together in a higher truth of genuine objectivity that can unify us into ever more efficient dealings with each other.

Part One of this book diagnoses the problem. Over-reliance on mechanical objectivity, while sidelining principle as optional, may have worked for the privileged in the sixteen to twentieth century colonial and neo-colonial worlds. It is a recipe for disaster in today's global economy. It leaves the people at the mercy of false-prophet demagogues. With self-centred post-truths, these whip up the masses to non-existent wonderlands, while scapegoating vulnerable outsiders as the reason for all that goes wrong.

Part Two defines a better way of doing business with each other, and then explores the benefits. By insisting upon evenly applied principles of kindness in all our dealings with friends, enemies, and strangers, we chart a path to transform post-truth into higher, unshakeable truth. This is the completely objective and efficient way to organise not only a successful economy but a happy life.

This fourth book of my **Astrological Quartet** draws upon four decades of studying world events and individual actions, using the insight and genuine objectivity provided by astro-event cycles and Buddha Dharma. Throughout this time my adolescent admiration for modern science and social idealism has not waned. If only these modern methods would complete themselves by welcoming in the incredible benefits of the ancient wisdoms that I have given the second half of my life to serve. Then we would have a higher-truth that saves us all!

Roy Gillett
January 2017

See the end of the book for more details of
Roy Gillett's *Astrological Quartet*.

Introduction - Wasted Years

This book started as a lament for the post-2008 years; wasted by the futility of conventional economists' 'prop up and plaster' attempts to sustain a bankrupt world economic system. Early in this writing it became clear that radical change was needed and this led to implications way beyond economics. So, this book has broadened into questioning the tenets of the main institutions that comprise our modern world. Having done so, it searches for core principles that are more than pleasant-sounding words to be accepted and then ignored. They must be real and effective, and applied consistently and uncompromisingly to every aspect of our lives, and to all our social institutions.

True principles point to consequences. If we wish to deny arms to brutal dictators, we may need to deny work to ordinary people engaged in arms manufacture. When condemning tax havens, should we not also deny ourselves the right to set the world's lowest rate of corporation tax? When expecting our politicians to look after our narrow interests, we should expect to be under attack from those who look after other people's interests. When we cheat to save our family, we must accept that others will cheat us for the same 'justifiable' reason. When offered something for nothing, seek assiduously for the hidden cost.

Since none of the above transactions are principled, they do not solve problems, but merely create more problems, more disappointment, disaffection, sense of betrayal and impotent helplessness. Do we really have to live in such a jaundiced, unprincipled world? Is this the harsh reality that those in power tell us we must 'knuckle under' and welcome their protection from?

Refusal to accept this in our hearts, and those of just about anyone hearing about this book, is the reason for it being written. It starts with an incisive exposé of the false philosophical assumptions of self-interest upon which contemporary economic theories rely. Then it exposes the consequent futility in every area of contemporary society: our rules and laws, the dysfunctional materialism of our knowledge and education systems; the disinterested manipulative inhumanity of our politicians and marketing experts; and our artists' neglect and prostitution of the very soul of our culture.

Strong words, which this book seeks not only to justify, but, in doing so, to find new resolute principles that could start a process of healing, leading to a system of real values. The book seeks not only a radically alternative approach to economic management, but principles to apply to our lives that nearly all religions and cultures could accept as an enlightened way of healing our relationships and our planet.

Failed economic assumptions the root of all problems
What follows then is an incredible journey of discovery. It starts with 'the money', where *Ecology Economy and Kindness*[2] left off in early 2009. As we struggled then to recover from the terrifying autumn 2008 world economic collapse, my book offered an incisive analysis of the system and strategies that had brought the world to this brink of chaotic disaster. It then warned against future errors that would lead to an even worse collapse, if replied upon.

> We can protect what we have and blame and attack others, accusing them of causing our problems. We can manipulate interest rates, money supply, extend debt, and seek to stimulate consumption in artificial and often unnecessary ways.[3]

While it went on to accept that 'Some elements of such short-term tricks may be needed to ease the transition to the third [efficiently principled] option' it is of fundamental concern that now, many years on, people in power continue to rely solely on such strategies, and to claim recovery is well on the way. But is this growth that brightens the lives of better-off countries and sub-groups sustainable? For an answer, we need to take our minds back to the feelings and actions when that autumn-2008 financial crisis burst upon the world. Readers of *Economy Ecology and Kindness* have always had that advantage. If you did not read it then, or have not recently, do so right away. It will put economic developments since then, and our understanding of today, in a stark, profoundly worrying perspective. For our economic mindsets and policy decisions since 2008 remain trapped within the two ineffective false choices described in the above quotation: to 'protect what we have, blame and attack others, accusing them of causing our problems.'

When our possessions and work, and the prosperity we enjoy from them, seem at risk, understandably we turn on those who encouraged our false expectations. We want to blame and punish those who gained for themselves by exploiting everyone's naivety; false prophet economists, fund managers, bankers and their incompetent regulators. Also in the frame are the politicians, who were all too happy to 'turn a blind eye', honour, reward and bask in the glory[4] of those they now condemn. Since 2008, a few have been 'fingered' and disgraced. Most remain, battered a little, maybe, but still very much in power. The system is resilient, because it has most of our resources under its control. It seems so crucial to our survival that we demand no more than minor ill-considered reforms!

After initial outrage, the search for scapegoats takes on a more sinister and far less logical course. Our problems are said to be caused by immigrant workers, membership of the European Union, unemployed 'scroungers' living off the backs of 'hard-working families'. Such simplistic analysis leads to piecemeal policy decisions, mostly counter-productive; at worst, downright insensitive and cruel. Punitive initiatives to get the young, disabled, both parents, indeed everyone, working, however low the wage, enriches employers and venture capitalists at the expense of the family life and happiness of ordinary people.

At the other extreme, we point to the aggressive avoidance strategies of multinational corporations, implying that changing the rules to 'ensure' they paid their share would make everything better. We shall see that this leads merely to the employment of brilliant legal minds to manipulate complex regulations. In this way, large commercial interests continue to gain financially, even when, if at all, the new rules are in place.

Blaming and scapegoating, however much the target deserves it, does not solve anything. It is not the people who exploit the system, but the system itself and our acceptance of it that bear the key responsibility for what happened in 2008 and will happen again and be even worse in the future.

'Manipulating interest rates and the money supply to extend debt, while seeking to stimulate consumption in artificial and often unnecessary ways', as we wait for the economic cycle to turn, show we do not even understand what is needed, let alone are ready to address it.

A sounder base for capitalism
Economy Ecology and Kindness went on to insist

> ... the real solution is to question assumptions that have brought us to similar predicaments for decades, even centuries. The economy is the way we manage material relationships. Because it is material, economic theory must follow the basic laws of physics — nothing is for nothing.[5]

and outline some broad principles that would be a genuine efficient new way of structuring world affairs. For it is genuine efficiency we must respond to, if we are to emerge happily from these Pluto in Capricorn[6] years.

Because little progress has been made since the 2008 wake-up call, we need to look in much more depth and detail to identify and answer the key areas of weakness in our current world system. This will take us well beyond economic argument into the very assumptions about the role of rules and law, how we discover and use knowledge, and how we communicate. We need far greater empathy in our relationships and efficiency in how we do business with each other.

The exploitative capitalist system, developed over the past 300 years, consists of powerful interdependent institutions. Their working together perpetuates difficult-to-breach assumed 'truths', against which radical questioning leading to real change seems well-nigh impossible. *Economy, Ecology and Kindness* identified a new *Gold Standard*, as an ideal concept[7] to cut through these defences and be a touchstone to assess whether proposals for change were real and sustainable. This book develops what this meant into a *Golden Standard* principle and applies it to clarify key world systems; showing how each can be cleansed to meet this *Golden Standard*.

Breaking the barriers to a better world
In today's hedonistic world, we expect answers to be fun and immediate, but such answers are short lived. As a trawler's net tightens, the small fish cannot avoid the gaping jaws of the larger ones, but wrenched from the water into the air and tossed upon the deck, those jaws remain open, frozen and unsatisfied, with smaller fish uneaten in their mouths. Today's pleasures are like this to individuals and peoples throughout the world. Easy prey in a net of simplistic solutions to promised plenty, they find themselves caught up in a tawdry, counterproductive hotchpotch of fear-driven small-minded defensive rules, prejudices and enforcement systems. Processes use greed to define and drive our differences, and fear to reinforce them. Decisions turn upon

whether 'the rules' were obeyed. Is that opinion worth listening to? Should everyone have a right to decide for themselves? Who should have permission to enter and reside? 'My right to bear or not to bear arms should exist above all else.' 'Those kinds of people and ideas are threatening.' 'Not everyone should be treated equally.' Listen to the 24-hour worldwide news; see its focus on what separates us from 'strangers' and the means to defend and make agreements to keep us 'safely' apart.

This current world psychosis has reached such a state of hysteria that it is considered the natural way of things. Thousands stand in the street to die, and men, women, even children, in desperation are driven to use themselves as human bombs, or travel thousands of miles to behead strangers. Instead of desperately seeking to hide from this, we should do more than gape open-mouthed, and look for evil manipulating groomers to blame. Until we look deep within ourselves to see the part we (not they) have played to bring the world to this, we will never see and address the fundamental cause. Quite simply, driven by unwarranted fear, we have gone to great lengths to create and keep in place unnecessary barriers between ourselves and others.

Barriers, be they physical, legal or social, are obstacles put up by those including ourselves in power to avoid facing up to the consequences of their exploitative injustices toward others. Seeing the decks stacked against them, those we shut out turn to increasingly desperate measures: law-breaking, people and substance smuggling, sabotage, terrorism, rejection of entire cultures, ethnic cleansing; all driven and sustained by narrow-minded educators, laws, social workers, law enforcers and armies.

Put all this paranoia to one side for a moment. Instead, visualise a world without barriers, where all are free to wander, work and live where they will. See a world where our policies and actions are moving in this direction; not constantly looking for reasons and putting in place strategies to defend against the 'danger' of such a possibility.

Impossible? Maybe, but only because we have come to seek refuge in pseudo-principles based on self-interest, rather than overriding principles of truth and honour that apply equally to all. Reliable principles that will make us safe are based on genuine give and take, where the truth is more important than any person or group; or even any rule and regulation. Only when we encourage decent respect and heartfelt principled concern for individuals and groups, the right of everyone to pursue health, wealth and happiness, can we come together safely, enshrining values we all share. The extent to which we cannot see and do this is the extent to which the world fails, not only morally and socially, but economically as well.

This is not woolly-minded, unrealistic idealism. On the contrary, it is an incredibly hard-headed realistic way of grounding our world economy and indeed all our dealings with each other. For there is no doubt that when people work together for a common cause, they give more, ask for less and take ever-greater pride in the endeavours they share with an increasingly varied body of friends. It is the key way of putting right our capitalist system — indeed, its salvation.

The Pluto-in-Capricorn cycle, with us until 2024, could perpetuate horror, failure, social decay and international conflict on an ever-worse scale. As we stand on the brink, will we do better than our sixteenth and eighteenth century forebears at not dissimilar times in the astro-cycles? Will we let go of assumptions of impossibility and struggle toward a more ideal world? In our heart of hearts every one of us wants to try hard to do just this; if not for us, for our children and those that come after them.

It is possible! The first seven chapters describe what is wrong; the next five how to put it right. Stay with and read all of them and learn how to make it better.

Part One

Ways to Global Destruction

Chapter 1
The 'Global Race' - the Problem not the Solution

For thousands of years, astrologers have used the interaction of the cycles between Jupiter and Saturn to understand the rise and fall of political and economic success.

The two represent opposing yet complementary forces. Jupiter, unrestrained on its own, describes a world instantly exploding in myriad pieces to infinitely faraway places in infinite directions. Saturn, on its own, describes a world firm-fixed in immovable impossibility. Of course, they are not alone, but work with each other and other astro-cycles.

When Jupiter moves through a zodiac sign the expansion in our lives takes on the qualities of that sign. Opportunities arise, doors open, we experience the generosity of its nature. By way of contrast, when Saturn passes through a zodiac sign, we are faced with that sign's realities, rules and structural requirements. Too much expansion becomes unstable, even destructive, while too much restriction leads to an unproductive lack of progress. Because of this, when the two forces work respectfully together, they can correct each other's excesses. Saturn steadies, structures and channels Jupiter's expansiveness. Jupiter stirs the static Saturn, creates opportunity where previously there was immobility and hopelessness.

The cycle of the two planets in the heavens means that they come together at a point in the zodiac once every twenty years and opposite each other at the ten years in-between. In current times, this means the conjunction occurs at or near the beginning of even decades (1980, 2000, 2020, etc.) and the opposition occurs at or near the beginning of odd decades (1970, 1990, 2010, 2030, etc.). After the two conjunct, Jupiter moves faster, taking just 12 years to transit the zodiac. It moves through signs ahead of Saturn, which takes 29+ years to complete the same journey. They wax further and further apart, until after ten years they are in opposite signs. Over the ten years from this point, Jupiter wanes ever closer to another conjunction to Saturn.

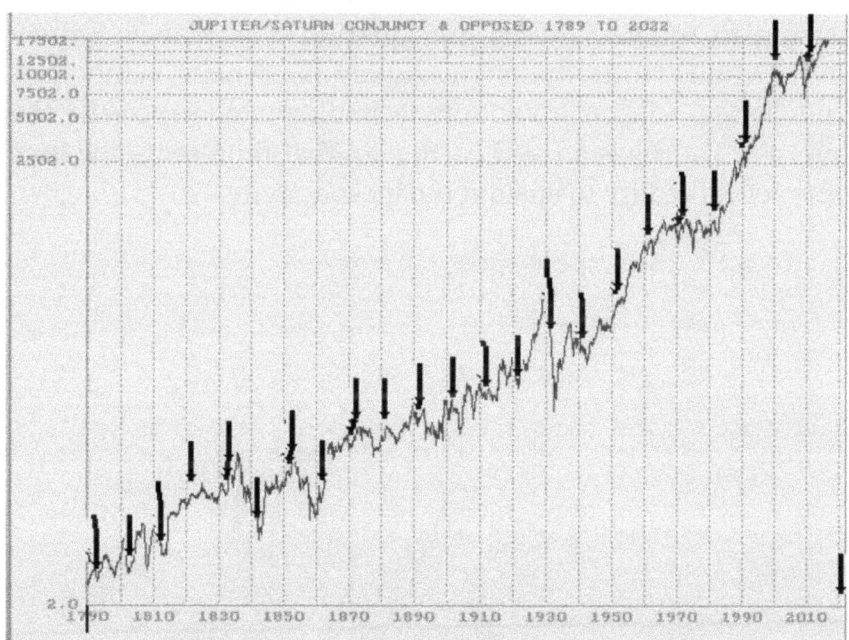

Reconstituted equities with DJIA from 1789
Prices logarithmically adjusted to allow for inflation

The groups of arrows in the diagram above show the conjunctions and then oppositions of the two planets alongside reconstituted equities with Dow Jones Industrial Index from 1789. It shows these planetary events are associated with major turns in the price level; see the Irish potato famine in 1840s, three oppositions in 1930 and many more. This is confirmed when we magnify it to focus on shorter periods of time. The diagram on the next page shows the last three decades in sharper contrast.

This shows that Jupiter-Saturn conjunctions and oppositions are frequently there when price growth reverses, even more so if you study the graph in the context of its contemporary price level.

When we consider other astro-cycles as well, the association becomes even more precise. The 2000 Dot-com bubble collapse was particularly strong, because the Jupiter Saturn conjunction occurred with up to five other bodies in Taurus closing to square Uranus in Aquarius. The planets Saturn and Uranus rule the sign Aquarius, which symbolises knowledge, science, invention, technology and especially the Internet. Taurus is a fixed earth sign that represents the love of practical reality to sustain business activity.

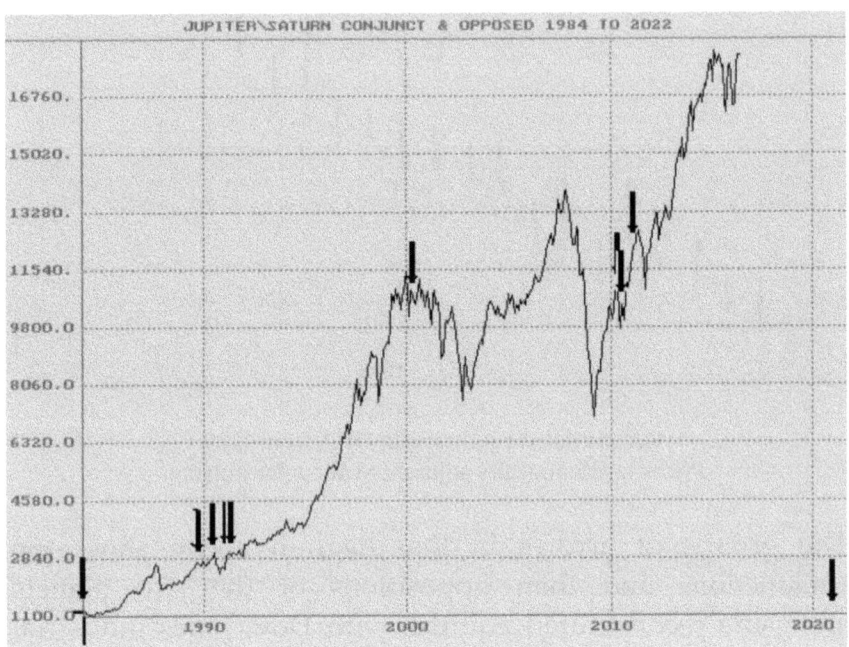

DJIA from 1984 - actual prices

The chaotic manipulative qualities of our current system, graphically described by both the Bank of England and US Federal Reserve horoscopes that we shall study in Chapter 2, are often constrained at times of strong earth planets. In 1929, Neptune entered the earth sign of Virgo in late July, just as the equities markets were slowing, after a massive Neptune-in-Leo equities boom. The exact peak was on the

3rd September Virgo New Moon day. From then, markets struggled to recover. Finally, they crashed in disastrous stages leading to Black Tuesday, 29th October. It was just a few months before Jupiter in Cancer opposed Saturn in the earth sign of Capricorn – 'the managing director of the universe'.

With up to five planets in the earth sign of Capricorn (including a rare 171-year Uranus-Neptune conjunction), the 1989-90 opposition saw the end of the Soviet state-capitalist system and a considerable downturn in free-enterprise markets too. The western system struggled to recover, but at the end of 1994, when Jupiter conjunct Pluto entered Sagittarius, markets spectacularly reversed upward to herald a period of irresponsible expansion, which accelerated into the 2000 Dot-com reversal, as Jupiter-Saturn conjuncted in Taurus and squared Uranus in Aquarius.

Now, several decades after that warning and even more seduced by expansion, we are applying ever more ingenious short-term strategies to 'avoid' the approaching confrontation with reality.

Consequences of ignoring the Jupiter-Saturn rhythm

Underlying not only economic activity, but all other events in our lives, is the Jupiter-Saturn twenty-year generational cycle. For the first ten years, it is easier to expand and possibly over reach. These are followed by a further ten years when it is best to consolidate. Unfortunately, the exploitative capitalist system that dominates our economy today seeks to avoid any hint of consolidation for all it is worth. We must expand, grow, win a race, be the best. Anything less is a failure, a problem to be worked around, by manipulating the money supply and equity values, delaying the timing of payments, creating false assets.

The sub-prime crisis that burst upon us in 2008 can be traced back to the 1980s deregulation policy that allowed various unwise manipulations of the markets over the intervening years.[8] Saturn's 2003-5 transit in detriment in Cancer clearly indicated that great care should be taken to avoid overheating and hence future problems in real estate. The financial institutions in the US, followed by those throughout the world, unwisely did the opposite and eased restrictions on loans. It was claimed that hedging strategies, such as Credit Default Swaps, could spread and so remove risk. Indeed, estimates of the value of such instruments being bought and sold was included in the profit and loss and balance sheets of companies, grossly inflating their trading and asset values. Traders received bonuses accordingly. Full details of many other false assumptions are fully explained in *Economy Ecology and Kindness*.

Such relentless, acquisitive greed is reminiscent of infestations in nature: ants to sugar, flies to food, field mice coming indoors for winter, rabbits multiplying when food is plentiful, infection in an open, untreated wound, influenza when the winter weather weakens our resistance. When conditions are right, these creatures take hold and multiply exponentially, until they have squandered all resources. Then their expansion becomes unsustainable. They fade away and die in a ravaged landscape.

With Pluto entering Saturn's sign in 2008, the consequences of all this delusion in economic markets were felt early, intensifying up to the 2010-11 Jupiter-Saturn opposition. Then, as so often in the past, correction was forced upon markets. By which time the consequences were far more dire than they would have been if, in accordance with the two planets' natural cycle, a proper voluntary correction had been made in good time.

We start to behave better than those mindless manifestations of the natural world when we use our intelligence and foresight to develop a system that welcomes built-in consolidation. Give, take and containment are not enemies to happiness, to be avoided at all costs. Nor are they tragedies when, refusing to be ignored, they burst in on us.

Our economic model seems to be based on a strategy of overeating until we are sick. We need a much better system than this; one based on so much respect for pleasure that we do not sully it with overindulgence.

Unfortunately, the core of our present system is to believe constraints of nature are avoidable, by passing the consequences of our excesses on to unsuspecting others. The most brilliant minds are rewarded for finding and implementing ingenious avoidance and redirection schemes. Jupiter-like economic expansion is sustained for a time, until it overreaches and everything falls apart. Surprised and disappointed by the Saturnian consequences, we pick ourselves up and patch up the injuries as best we can; ready, as soon as possible, to apply Jupiter again. Nothing is learned. Saturn is Satan and seen as the enemy. It represents all the things and people we do not like, and will do everything we can to be rid of.

Believing in something better
Why do we continue to behave this way despite all those dire consequences: booms and busts, foreclosures, social unrest, clear injustice between rich and poor and international conflict? Why do we allow less deserving manipulators and exploiters to rule and receive the awards, while the kindest and purest receive no more than patronising gratitude from those on high?

Very few want it to be this way. Most feel we are obliged to believe what we are told: that this is 'the unavoidable way of the world'. Accepting this without question, we align ourselves to life patterns that seem to confirm it. We relegate and dismiss as weakness any regretful yearning deep in our hearts that wants it to be otherwise.

We acquiesce in an exploitative capitalist system that is the product of an integrated self-confirming network of institutions. These reach into and control <u>every aspect</u> of our lives: the lessons we learn at school and submit to at university; the devotion we are taught to have toward things rather than feelings and responsibilities; the way we submit to seductive persuasion, to triggers of greed and self-interest, to experts who promise to look after our every need; how we allow ourselves to be frightened and manipulated into accepting rules that give the haves more rights than the have nots; the way that we seek justice through rules that come too late and are avoided by profiteers; those in academia and financial regulation who sell out to the system of persuaders, experts and many politicians. All of them seem to tell us the same story about the same unavoidable reality that dictates 'it has to be like this', reassuringly saying 'we will do all we can for you, if you support us'.

Crucially, like the queen bee in a hive, they also tell us that we must work ever-harder to grow our economies, urge us to join in and help our group win the race! Unfortunately, it is a race to global destruction, because reality does not work that way. Nor do the kinds of science and social organisation that support that way do more than devise short-term distortions, seeking to get around the unavoidable reality of nature.

A systematic study of each area of society that creates and controls this destructively deluded world picture will reveal the incredibly incompetent contribution each of them makes. It will reveal that they are barriers to efficiency, not its custodians.

Today, substantial improvements in our living standards, expectancy and quality of life, brought to us by the scientific discoveries of the Industrial Revolution, are not dependent upon Jupiter-only-based speculative and exploitative capitalism. They needed, and always will need, a shape, a framework, a yielding-in as well as projecting-out, absorption as well as growth, reconciliation as well as assertion, space and time for renewal, fertilisation, putting in as well as taking out. It is not just about growth at any price, but sustainable growth, achieved by welcoming good order and consolidation. We need a Saturnian structural system for renewal that ensures we make maximum continuing use of Jupiter's riches, while honouring Saturn's key lessons. In our economic system, and everything we do, we must wish for and honour structure, limitation and consolidation as much as we celebrate opportunity, growth and new discovery.

As in work and economics, so it is in everything we do with each other. Balance and integrity should apply to our rules and laws and how we structure knowledge. As well as how we organise business, the balance of appropriate give and take should be in our personal relationships with friends and family. The wish to give as well as take should apply in political and other systems of communication, and especially in how we relate to the planet and its peoples. This is the way to happiness in everything we do.

Our times force us to change
Of course, such thoughts and words have been taught and ignored for millennia. Why should today be any different? Because today is different! Increasing consumption and populations demand a new way of looking at and organising the world. Science has given us the power to destroy the planet by explosion, or by eating it alive. Yet, we also have the means of communication through the World Wide Web and travel to know and act as one. By intelligent examination, cleansing of all our systems is possible. The more we understand and succeed in this, the happier we will be. These Pluto-in-Capricorn years are holding us to this task of true efficiency. We will be corrected by suffering every time we turn away from it.

Chapter 2 - The Problem with Economics

When practised without ethical foundation, free enterprise assumes that resources are limitless, or that ever-expanding scientific discoveries will find alternatives when supplies run out. Therefore, humanity has the right to exploit people, animals, nature and the very fabric of the planet for the greatest possible profit. Any shortfall in resources will be temporary and soon solved by future technical advances.

The world economic system that has developed over the past three centuries is intrinsically flawed, because it is based on such over-optimism. The problem is not capitalism (or free individual enterprise), but rather the brutally selfish way it has been practised from the very beginning, into the consequent monster of overproduction it has become today.

Post-2008 attempts to prop up, restart, sustain and accelerate growth will in the end make matters worse. They merely put off the time of reckoning and create a dangerous increase in gaps between rich and poor within countries and massive movements of populations between trading areas.[9]

The astrology chart for a key day in the foundation of our present world economic system clearly reveals that intrinsic flaws were there from the very beginning of modern capitalism. They have bedevilled its development ever since.

The chart drawn for noon on the day of the sealing of the Bank of England Royal Charter[10] on 27th July 1694 has Pluto, Sun and Jupiter close together in Leo. Mercury towards the end of the sign is trined to Saturn in Sagittarius. Considered together these factors suggest self-centred risky speculation; what control there is being in the service of personal gain. The mutable grand cross from that Saturn to Mars in Virgo, Neptune in Pisces and Venus conjunct Uranus in Gemini depicts duplicity. Also, any attempt at such control will be temporary and ineffective. Markets will have a mind of their own and constantly strive against restriction. The mutability may enable many approaches to work for a

The Problem with Economics

time, but continued success is dependent upon there being new fields to conquer. Moon in Libra T-square nodal axis suggest that enterprises will be carried forward with anxious instability.

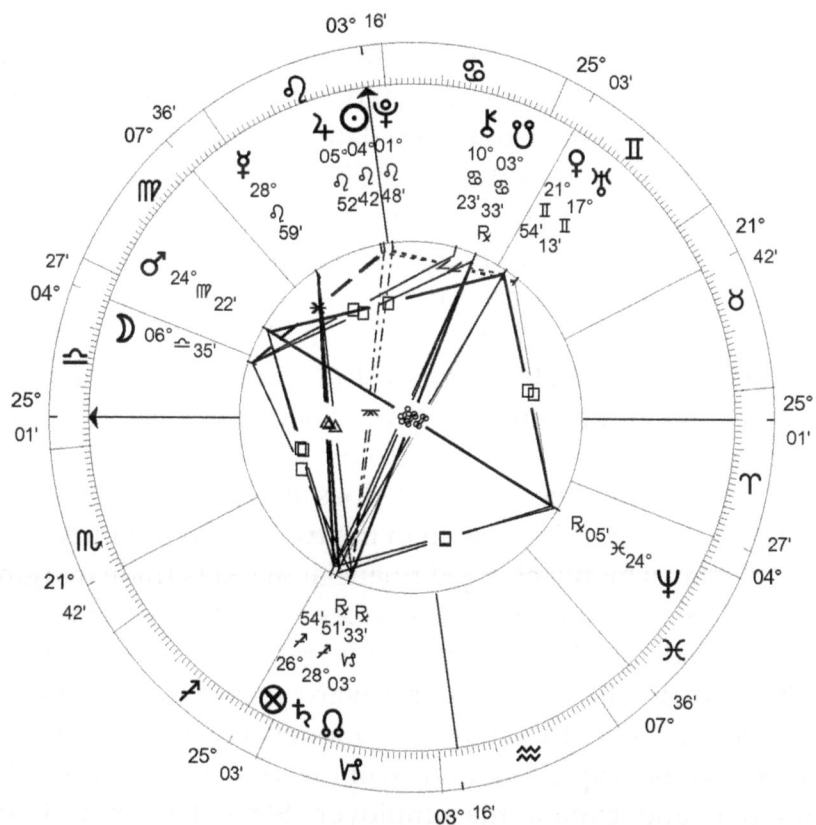

Bank of England
Noon LMT 27th July 1694 London, England

Packed with so much possibility, the new institution was highly successful. Investors received their promised return. The British Navy was rebuilt and restored to even greater status; to 'rule the waves' for two hundred years. Using share issues to raise capital for other enterprises became increasingly popular. Despite the warning signs of the South Sea Bubble debacle[11], speculative investment, often based on illusory collateral support, became the foundation of the rapidly expanding Industrial Revolution.

Personal gain the essential aim
The intrinsic nature and aim of the system is the manipulation of resources and information to produce a narrow focus of personal profit. Its success depends upon the existence of virgin resources and other people (suppliers, workers or customers) to manipulate and exploit.

This undermines the generally accepted justification of capitalism that workers and investors both contribute and gain equally in a joint enterprise. The investor provides the workplace and resources for the worker to labour and earn an income. With an empty Aries in the 6th house and its ruling Mars in the 11th, opposed to Neptune in Pisces in the 5th, the Bank of England chart describes enterprise where the workers are far removed from such an ideal. While employment may be a part, it does not have to be, and is increasingly becoming less so in the twenty-first century.

Today's highly charged financial markets trade margins rather than material resources. Computer-generated mechanised production radically reduces labour forces. Where work still is done, fair reward may not be central to the model. For, to satisfy the model, the worker should expect to be exploited and will, if possible, reverse the situation and exploit the employer. Slave labour and the blackmail of threatened industrial action walk hand-in-hand, casting a constant shadow over industrial relations!

While customers may be motivated to maintain patronage if satisfied with the product purchased, how they will be satisfied is not defined. The exploitative personal interest of this model of capitalism will be successful if the customer is tricked, coerced, tempted, even profiteered, into purchasing all, if not more than, he genuinely needs. The key definition of success is that everyone involved should accept, without question, circumstances by which investors continue to profit as much as possible.

Unethical profit motivation

Because there are no value judgements, or ethical standards built into the system, should society want them, they have to be introduced from outside. The successful entrepreneur will see codes and conditions enforced by such laws or customs as alien, unprofitable restraints. He will either find ways to avoid or turn them to personal profit. They will be treated as if they were constraints of the natural world, or demands of the labour force. It is claimed that the profit motivation leads to efficiency, because it stands and falls upon customer reaction to competitive pricing and quality. Yet, access to information about goods and services depends upon who controls the money market and/or manipulates the legalities. Because personal profit is the intrinsic aim, while quality and value (be they perceived or genuine) may help if they develop an expanding customer base, the most profitable way to manipulate circumstances will be the most sought after. When profits are based on illusory, short-term manipulations of the markets (especially the financial markets), players will flock to gain personal advantage. In this way booms are created. When they burst, the very nature of the system means that those who have gained most are unlikely to be the losers. Quite the opposite, the victims will be the 'Johnny come lateles' or, even more likely, those who did not understand what was happening and were never involved in the market in the first place.

When profit is the enemy of an efficient economy

In 1913, after a major boom and bust a few years earlier, the US Federal Reserve was founded to stabilise the markets, to defend investors and the population affected by their decisions. Despite its existence, the Neptune in Leo boom of the 1920s burst less than three months after that planet's July 1929 ingress into Virgo.

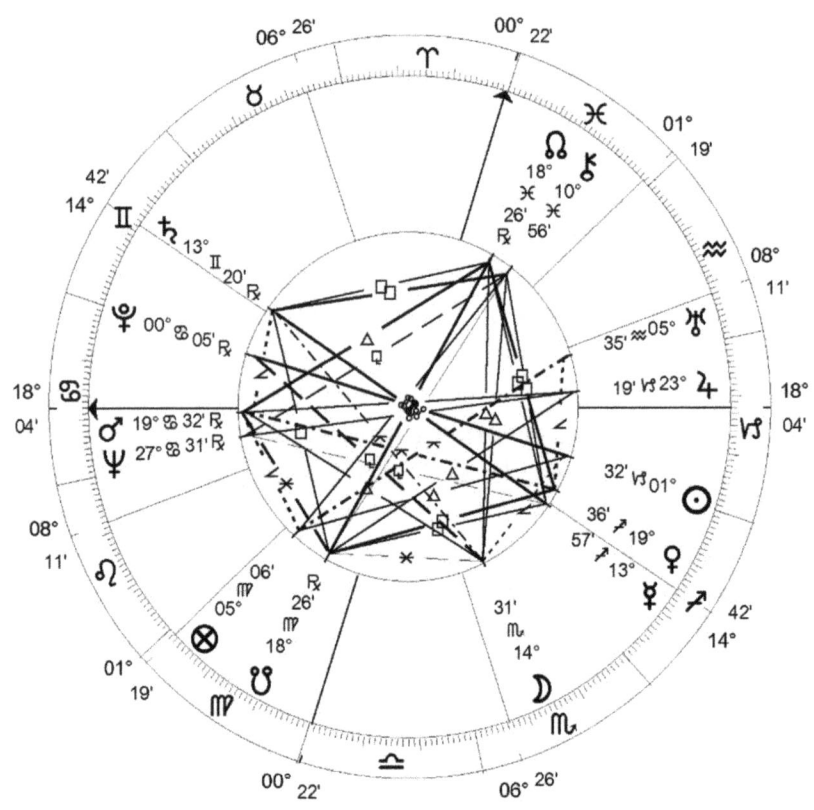

US Federal Reserve
1802 EST 23rd December 1913 New York, US

The reason the US Federal Reserve was unable to avert the crash and the traumatic 1930s recession that followed can be clearly seen from its foundation chart. Like the Bank of England, it has a grand cross. It is mutable involving the Pisces-Virgo nodal axis, with Chiron in Pisces, while Saturn in Gemini, opposed by Mercury conjunct Venus in Sagittarius, is on the other axis. So, the indications are similar. The chart suggests mixed messages and manipulatively deceptive information through lack of proper controls. Vulnerable expansive anxiety is suggested by Mars conjunct Neptune in Cancer opposed Jupiter in Capricorn across the ascendant-descendant axis. Also, the Sun makes a frightening opposition to Pluto across the Capricorn-Cancer cusps. The Moon forming a grand trine with Mars-Neptune and North Node-Chiron suggests passionate emotional intensity. The organisation is not there to care for the people and business, or even the market. It is there to control and manipulate desire, to enable the free cut and thrust of profit-taking. When this breaks down, it will manipulate to restore speculative profit and loss as soon as possible, whatever the cost to the people involved and the economies that so many other people depend upon.

In short, the system is not there to regulate and sustain good business, rather it is there as an amoral casino with a series of rules that can be worked around, but whose central aim is to facilitate winners and losers, whatever the rights and wrongs of what happens may be. It offers tempting, almost unbelievable riches and amazing highs for some for a while, amidst incredible risk and a near cavalier attitude (even disregard) toward long-term consequences. For where does the chart point to this being the concern or responsibility of the main players?

The nemesis of exploitative capitalism

Frighteningly, this is the economic system that was exported to most of the world by the rich colonial powers. Here it meets a nemesis, from which all of us are increasingly suffering. The model is based on the exploitation of virgin resources and innocent cultures. So, what happens now that fewer and fewer of these remain? Not only do we face global warming and an energy crisis, but, quite simply, we are running out of speculative investment opportunities to colonise. Increasingly, entrepreneurs are being forced to exploit each other; like snakes in a dank, crowded, equatorial jungle; pressed, coiling around and feeding upon their neighbours. Dangers become ever more sudden and frequent, as room for manoeuvre lessens.

Globalisation

It was not meant to be this way, but globalisation has accelerated this process. Intent on immediate gain, and ignoring long-term consequences, the captains of western exploitative capitalism jumped at the possibility of opening access to vast new markets in emerging economies. With the barriers to global trade coming down, the emerging nations mastered and improved on western technology. With low labour costs, they could supply the Old World at dramatically reduced prices.

Owners of western companies were happy to profit, by moving production off-shore to be delivered by the rapidly expanding enterprises in the emerging countries. Enabling cheaper prices for customers and increased profits for the company, it seemed like a win-win situation; except, that is, for the workers in western countries.

For some time, globalisation seemed to be benefiting everyone. It was good to see poor countries progressing, to have wonderful products at lower-than-ever prices. Most peoples' economies seemed to be growing. Those made redundant in the old industries were well compensated and could move to the now expanding service areas of the economy.

China joining the World Trade Organisation in 2001 dramatically expanded capacity at even lower prices. With rising asset values, providing collateral for readily available credit, all seemed good until 2008.

Since then, the reality of what globalisation run by exploitative capitalism means for most people has become painfully apparent. Incomes and rights at work have been largely lost, as workers are told this is the only way to compete with emerging countries. As well as loss of work opportunity and security, financial austerity has led to shortages in health, housing and welfare support.

Unease in international social and religious relations leading to a massive world refugee problem has combined with financial uncertainty to fuel intolerance and conflict within nations. While we constantly bemoan the consequences, we nearly always misunderstand the root cause. We are floundering amidst an unavoidable massive re-distribution of world wealth, to redress the balance after centuries of colonial exploitation. The originators of globalisation may have had higher motivation than mere short-term personal gain, but they have unleashed unsustainable, post-colonial counter consequences that are changing the world order and the way we do business with each other.

By trying to base this massive global economic change on a financial system long past its sell-by date, we dispossess ordinary western citizens, while enabling a privileged minority to enjoy unjustifiable profit. To sustain this outmoded business structure, people throughout the world are urged to work ever harder to win a global race to ever more consumption, propped up by illusory credit.

Globalisation may be what a good healthy global village needs, but only if based on a much better system of values than this.

The built-in failure of short-term strategies
Present strategies avoid, rather than address, what is needed. With most fixed assets spent by the end of the 1980s, monetarist economists employed creative accounting. When artificially low interest rates became ineffective in the early twenty-first century, they turned to the spending of non-existent assets. Banks generated expansion by encouraging credit card holders to transfer their debt balances, interest-free from one card account to another. Then they did the same with each other by trading an uncontrolled market of

debt insurance schemes, such as Credit Default Swaps. Within a few years, nominal risks were worth far more than the entire world economy. Read or re-read *Economy Ecology and Kindness*[12] where a full explanation of the nature and astrology behind these monumental self-deceptions is explained.

Have we learnt and changed our ways since 2008? Apparently not! Rather, to perpetuate the system for a few more years, world economists and politicians have taken the sadly futile and counterproductive path that *Economy Ecology and Kindness* specifically warned against. They have been 'manipulating interest rates and the money supply, extending debt, seeking to stimulate consumption in artificial and often unnecessary ways.'[13] All of which has and can do no more than close a few gaps while opening others. Fundamentally, this will change and solve little. It will do no more than prop up the same intrinsically flawed system.

How long can growth last?
Gulf states are rich with petrol money for now. In 2016, London and New York may enjoy short-term prosperity, based on artificial financial trading advantages. Rich speculators may tuck away capital there, because these are in the best present places for speedy asset gains — especially in property — until the bubble bursts!

How sustainable and securely founded is the growth of Chinese production? This is the key question for the whole world. Ironically, today the Chinese middle classes are sustaining western economies by importing from them. However, China's appetite for consumption is no more infinite than the rest of the world's. Since the 2008 economic collapse, the US economy has been sustained by increasing its government debt from just under eleven trillion to more than nineteen trillion dollars. Nearly all world economies have seen the percentage difference between such debt and Gross National Product GDP increase by massive percentages. Should the rapid growth of emerging economies run out of steam, what will prop up the world economy, expanding debt exposure? Indeed, China is sustaining its growth by accumulating a 'very high mountain of debt'.[14] All Chinese debt government, financial, corporate and domestic increased by 381% between 2007 and 2014. In 2015 the country's total debt was 250% of its GDP.[15] Amidst amazing growth and prosperity, the Chinese property boom has led to ghost towns in some areas. Will international, combined with domestic, demand ever be sufficient to consume products and sustain ever-growing capacity? In September 2016, Ken Rogoff, a former IMF Chief Economist, said of the Chinese economy that 'a calamitous 'hard landing' for one of the main engines of global growth could not be ruled out. I think the economy is slowing down much more than official figures show.'[16]

Whether or not expansion will be more short-term than generally accepted, how much longer will people be encouraged to work harder for low wages? Will they be content to give over family life to government-approved carers? We are bruising the planet with heavy-handed technology, squeezing out what remains of fossil fuels. These are the last desperate 'throws of the dice' of a system dangerously past its sell-by date.

The futility of short-term economic 'sticking plasters'
The astro-cycles underlying the present decade explain why it is tempting to continue to seek short-term, seemingly easy ways out of crisis. Neptune with Chiron in Pisces represents a yearning for healing, understanding and empathy, modified by the youthful, inexperienced revolutionary driving force of Uranus in Aries. Together they suggest there must be an easy answer that is kind to as many people as possible. 'Why not look only for pleasant solutions, focus on getting by in the present. The economic cycle will turn of its own accord; the future will look after itself.'

We have seen that on such assumptions banks, even some governments, have been bailed out. Central banks extended favourable terms of credit to both. The European Central Bank has gone further, by guaranteeing it will buy Italian and Spanish government bonds (debt) at a manageable, low rate, should it ever be speculated against. The strategy of reducing bank interest rates to encourage consumption, so successful in the 1990s, was no longer effective. So, a system of Quantitative Easing (QE) was tried. This involves central banks creating money by buying securities, such as government bonds, from banks, with electronic cash that did not exist before. The idea is that the private bank's enhanced balance sheet can then be used to finance loans to customers and hence stimulate the economy. They can also build their own assets, by investing in and so enhancing the value of equities they already possess.

Giving custodianship of the stimulus resources money that has no intrinsic existence to the very people who have shown themselves to trade aggressively in their own self-interest could lead to dire long-term consequences. Short-term purchases of assets may temporarily push up stock and bond prices, but only as long as there is new money coming in. Because of this, QE strategy risks creaming off funds merely to force up asset prices, when they were really intended to provide loans to enable genuine long-term business investment. Any short-term stimulus caused by a temporary rise in equity values is an incidental spin-off, leading to no more than unsustainable temporary capital gains for the few. Financial traders become constantly hungry beggar kids, waiting for the next cash hand-out; hardly an efficient way of regenerating the world economy!

The nemesis of self-deception
Once again, (un)fortunately, we have to consider Pluto in Capricorn. So far, the wide-ranging authoritarian transformation required in our world economy has merely

knocked at the door of those held to be responsible for its shortcomings. Radical change has not been considered. Ways to do not more than introduce a few rules and plug loopholes in the system have merely been discussed. To date, the targeting of the financial institutions that encouraged and presided over the collapse of the system has been long in coming and minor in redress. Banks have been obliged to repay considerable amounts for misselling, but only a few low-level traders have been prosecuted. The focus seems to have been on pre-arranged out of court fines; a petty thief would not be so lucky! Such gestures of punishment do not prevent the institutions and the system itself from passing on the fines to customers, finding new employees and continuing with business as usual. Financially over-extended individuals or those with shares, pensions, or employment dependant on financial markets have felt the full force of Pluto in Capricorn. Many have lost their homes, assets, pensions or jobs – some all four. Attempts to bring in rules for the future have been protracted. Those they are aimed at will find new ways to avoid them by the time they are in force.

Even if these minor actions were to be implementable they would be peripheral to the radical changes needed. As the Jupiter-Saturn cycle builds through its waning phase to join Pluto in Capricorn from 2018 and especially in 2020, the period[17] demands a much more radical change in the rules of the world economy. Our facile-so-far ('weedy') efforts to answer the force of Capricorn demand will bring constant failure and disappointment. Do we have to descend to the very root of real death to force effective Capricorn structural rigour upon our dealings?

Pluto's last Capricorn transit (1762-78) occurred in the early Industrial Revolution. The developments in those years were to change the very basis of authority and start the expansion to a very different world. Industrialisation and expanding transport systems were to free people to travel.

New-money entrepreneurs were to replace a privileged aristocracy and absolute monarchies. Ordinary people struggled for political rights, as populations moved away from peasantry and cottage industries.

Consider the difference between then and now, and then visualise a similar dimensional leap from the twenty-first century Pluto transit through Capricorn into a global society accessed via a World-Wide-Web. Consider the impact of computerised production, three-dimensional printing and nanotechnology. Through the past 300 years, the value systems held before the seventeenth and early eighteenth centuries struggled to understand, address and adapt to the rapid change that scientific invention, technology and social upheaval was to bring to people's lives. Equally inadequate for us now is today's outmoded world economic and political system designed for those colonial times, when vast virgin areas of the world were there to be explored and exploited. How can it be good enough now that so little remains to be plundered?

Exploitative marketing, based on intensive cheap labour production by emerging Chinese and other Asian economies may be bringing major improvements in methods and quality. However, resources are finite, as the Chinese rush for the rights over raw materials in Africa and South America shows. The rest of us are left to asset-strip in the remaining enterprises. We manipulate and plunder vulnerable businesses, use negative interest rates to encourage people to spend, squeezing out what easy wealth remains. Russia and Canada drill for oil deep down under Arcstic ice, and most of the rest of us continue rather mindlessly to demand no interruption to our energy-greedy lives. The wise will see time rapidly running out, if we are to avoid the nonsense of eating our planet alive!

None of this will work for long. Tension for real change will build, as the 2018-24 Capricorn focus puts us through truly challenging consequences, forcing implementation of radical change.

A better system of enterprise
Fascinating alternatives arise if we refuse to be defeated by the Capricorn confrontation with reality, and instead allow globalisation to force change for the better upon us.

When resources become scarce, we can gain by: making technological advances that are less energy-demanding; finding ways of using and producing less and re-using more; making fewer journeys; having less lighting, better heating and insulation.

Do we have to work so many hours and spend such little quality time with our loved ones; leaving them to be raised in state-run or financed pre-, after- and holiday-schools? With more time at home, we would buy less, make and repair more – insist that products we do need are accessible and made to last. The extent and quality of relationships with and support between neighbours would grow. By living within, rather than ever aspiring to live beyond, our means, we discover our true nature and learn what we really want. Giving ourselves the space for the pace of life to settle; being free of constant obligation; having the time to discover the real priorities; these are the ways to find and become our real selves. Then we will have something of our own to work for and protect.

Of course, this would involve letting go of much that the system tells us (in its own interests) we cannot do without. It involves being courageous, open to considering the consequences of economic organisation that is based upon ethical foundations. It requires a change in mindset, to realise that real efficiency is incompatible with self-interest. Real, lasting efficiency relies upon what is right for all, now and in the future. It comes from refusing to believe promises that, in our heart of hearts, we know will never be met and we never wanted in the first place. It requires us to stop being taken in by easy answers that constantly let us down, and so lead to 'jaundiced' cynicism about everything and everyone in power.

Such a change involves the questioning not only of our economic assumptions and practices, but of all the interconnected institutions that underpin them. If economics needs to be based on more than greed, then the rules and principles of how we are with each other need a major re-think. How we learn, know and teach about our society needs to be questioned. The motivations behind the way we communicate and deal with each other need to be cleansed.

The next chapter starts by rigorously questioning how we decide and administer right and wrong.

Chapter 3 - The Problem with Rules and the Law

The true etymology of the word Universe means only one, infinite, all-inclusive, unending space, time and possibility, with no thing or possibility excluded, or not excluded.

By taking up a position or perspective within that Universe, we impose a limited relative reality upon it. That reality is dependent on how we assume our own identity and so see within its limitation. By saying what we think is true, we say more about ourselves than we do about the Universe. To cats, dogs, birds, creatures living at the bottom of the deep dark ocean, the bacteria within and dependent upon our bodies, the 'entire Universe', as they see it, is radically different to how we see it. Yet, are not all these views real to the beholder?

Imagine a being so enormous as to encompass far, far further and more of the Universe than our instruments can see and hear, a being in proportion far larger than we are to the bacteria within our bodies, a being to whom the Big Bang and all that came after is no more than the flick of a switch. How could we understand such a being or the rules that determine its existence?

Because everything is possible, subject to conditions which are dependent upon ourselves, then anything we are convinced is true is merely a projection of ourselves. We create our own reality by imposing certain conditions, measurements and judgements upon what we decide will be our environment. Maybe our home and family, our community, country, planet, systems of observation and knowledge, even what we consider to be the 'whole Universe'. The Large Hadron Collider is no more than the mechanical implementation of an enthusiasm shared by a large group of highly intelligent and skilful people. Studying the Universe in this way may bear brilliant fruit that will change millions of lives for good or ill, but it is not as close to *absolute* truth as the experience of two young lovers finding each other for the first time.

The mass deceptions of 'absolute truths'
Yet in nearly every culture throughout the ages of human existence, and maybe in many other beings and worlds where consciousness resides, groups tend to decide and behave as though theirs was the only universal reality. Then they make rules to perpetuate the security of their identity within that reality.

Religions and philosophies seek to explain ultimate realities and to dictate responsibilities and happy ways to 'the good life', as they see it. Some co-exist, others proselytise, insisting upon the exclusivity of their 'truth'. Social groups gather by sexual orientation (hetero-, homo-, bi- or trans-),[18] or enthusiasm for sport, music, dance, the countryside and so on and on. Bees and ants devote themselves to the growth of their colonies, seeing their queen as the undeniable source of goodness and life. Humans 'hover' around celebrities, avidly following their every move, living their own lives through them. Identities are reinforced by things that we must have for the sake of economic 'success'. Objects become associated with these cultures. Clothes, dress codes, homes, sounds, habits and mannerisms, ways of moving and listening and speaking and spending, all combine to make up complete life-style realities.

These 'realities' drive the priorities of our lives; from pay day loans to pay for children's Christmas presents (even maybe Premier League match tickets!) all the way to spending billions of dollars on armaments to wage wars 'to protect our way of life'. Caught up in what is important to us, we fail to see the larger picture of the world as other people view it. We may sympathise with their hardships and try to help in little ways. Yet in our heart of hearts, we see their way of life, not our own actions towards them, as the cause of their suffering. In this way, our way becomes the only way.

Failing to see from outside ourselves leads to ever greater errors and problems. The more we believe and insist on our view of reality, or path toward it, the greater the misunderstanding and conflict. This is how it happens:

- ❖ Religious devotion can excite and cleanse us into letting go enough to open a window to the truth underlying all things, the essential ultimate harmony of the Universe that allows all to be as it has, is and always will be.

    Both before and after such intimate recognition comes great danger! The calm point at the eye of a storm may be clear and quiet, but at the eye's immediate periphery the wind blows strongest and most dangerously. In our spiritual lives, having touched what we feel (and priests tell us is God), being reassured and feeling all is more right and wonderful than we dared to hope, comes the anxious question 'how long will it last?' How to protect what we have? Shall we fight to recover the joy? Do we bolster our devotion by seeking to convert others? So, around devotion swell great storms of potential disaster. When confidence in the future fails, we can be tossed and torn apart, love turns to hating those who disagree with our religious group. Wondrous contact with the still oneness of existence fades into grasping, and then sours to disastrous religious conflict and persecution. 'The medicine itself is turned into a poison.'[19]

- ❖ Cultural attachment: being in the company of people with common interests reinforces our identity. Knowing where we stand, feeling supported, strengthens our capacity to act; seems to make life easier and more productive. Being with like-minded people can be such fun!

    Working together and group loyalties are invaluable, but both can lead to problems when groups come to consider they alone are custodians of the one true answer. No path of race, belief, or sexual orientation need be celebrated or encouraged on its own; rather it is the capacity for unifying love that can be expressed in any path that we should value. Within public schools, inner city gangs, Rastafarian groups, tennis clubs, football supporters, fund-raising committees, people in our favourite pub, traditional Islamic women's groups, Soho strip club dancers and redneck voters, we will find qualities of loyalty, kindness to each other and closely guarded high principles of behaviour. What is considered the kind respect that members should hold for one another in each dramatically dissimilar cultural group is the basis of each group's security. The kind hospitality found in a gun-carrying small-town Texan community is not much different to that of a traditional community in the Middle East. Yet the labels of Christian and Muslim, American and Arab, make most people in each community see the other as alien enemies.

Rules and laws that divide
While only an extreme anarchist would deny a society's need for a code of conduct, far too many of us accept the laws and rules of our society without considering the consequences. Clearly laws based on knee-jerk reactions to tragic events can be counterproductive, but established rules can be equally ineffective, even divisive. Far too many are based on the dominant sub-group's view of reality. Sensing danger in the unfamiliar, they wish to protect themselves, their way of life, their very understanding of reality. Many may feel that a righteous wish to guide others away from the 'error of their ways' is a kindness, offered 'for their own good'.

The key test of any law is its acceptability. If the majority reject it, enforcement becomes problematic, even impossible. Even if it does gain majority support, minority groups will be marginalised, policing costs excessive and social unrest unending. Laws seeking to control business procedures can become artificial structures for the unscrupulous to overcome and profit from. Government consultation telegraphs new controls so far ahead of implementation that, by the time they are in place, ways of avoidance have been established and the 'field of play' has moved on.

Legal process can be fraught with misunderstanding, feelings of injustice and resentment. The English and Welsh Civil Procedure Rules (and similar systems in other lands) are an immensely complicated adversarial framework that can be used more to frustrate resolution and create misunderstanding than to resolve it.

The criminal process can be equally fraught. The majority feel the offence deserves punishment, yet a sizeable minority may disagree and feel ignored. Worst of all, most serious offenders are more likely to be supported by their social sub-groups – a 'them and us' atmosphere is created.

Catching, charging and punishing wrongdoers is time-consuming and expensive. Rules and laws are dependent upon the power of the law-maker to enforce them. The more laws, the more difficult is this process of enforcement and the more alienating and stressful for the police. Those in power can select which laws to enforce, leaving those not in power unprotected; even the victims of the laws of their lands. Laws to prohibit the use of alcohol and other recreational drugs over the past hundred years show this clearly. The more oppressive the enforcement, the greater is the opportunity for criminal profit, so vast that it can even finance international terrorism. Consumers threaten and steal from others to pay their dealers. The combined cost of enforcing the alcohol-drug laws and dealing with the consequent crime wave escalates. Combating the trafficking distorts cultural relations, both within and between the producing countries and consumer nations. Since these substances alter minds in very different ways, the case for specific drug laws is often a patronising power-play, seeking to push the kind of society the dominant group wish to live in. This may well depend upon which drugs (legal or illegal) each group uses.[20] Rarely, if at all, is all this about intrinsic right and wrong.[21] By trying to force one way we squander billions of dollars, ruin many lives and cultures in a desperate attempt to continue to misunderstand each other.

In the world of sport, the use of banned performance-enhancing substances is an ongoing issue. High-profile cases have disgraced past hero champions. In 2015, retrospective re-testing put the whole scrutiny process into question. What is and is not illegal can change. In 2016, Maria Sharapova's tennis career was interrupted when it was revealed she had continued to take a medicine, re-classified and banned for athletes earlier that year. Her behaviour had not changed. Yet now a chorus of frenetic self-righteous indignation from fellow athletes and sponsors called her a cheat, but only from the beginning of 2016!

This example shows that training for high-profile competitive sport is not always about playing fair or not playing fair, but rather about which substances and techniques are acceptable. The adulation that comes with sporting success is fickle, based as much on using special allowed substances and food diets to the limit, alongside straining the body with intensive training. All such competitions require unnatural behaviour; the greater the success the more intense the training. Perhaps events where specific substances are encouraged would add to the public entertainment – orienteering for LSD users comes to mind!

Far too often we are divided from each other by unfair, self-righteous overreaction to rules and regulations based on arbitrary criteria.

Rules as statements of social fashion
This is especially sad, because the enforcement, even the enactment, of many laws is often more about social fashion

than intrinsic integrity. In socially-unequal Victorian England, the rights of property owners were so prized that the starving poor could be imprisoned or transported for stealing a loaf of bread. In the 1940s and 1950s, grammar school pupil rugby players were initiated into singing songs about buggery and paedophilia. By 2015, a leading UK police chief trailed a policy for less police emphasis being placed on burglary, and funds being diverted to current and historic child abuse investigations. Until the 1960s homosexuality was a crime. Today in the UK, any discrimination-based sexual orientation is a crime. In the 1960s and 70s, corporal punishment was still practised in schools and anyone could have access to the care of children. In 2015, teachers touch a child at their peril, even if the touching is for the child's immediate protection. Could the zodiac sign occupied by Uranus in the birth charts of policemen and society's leaders indicate the change of emphasis? Defensive cover-ups suit Uranus in Cancer (people born 1949-55). The proud protection of children is suited to Leo, the Uranus sign of today's emerging leaders (born 1955-62). Their junior colleagues with Uranus in Virgo or Libra (born 1962-69 or 1969-76) are left to analyse the minutiae of the past behaviour and bring those responsible to justice.

The enactment and enforcement of new laws is nearly always dependent on the outcome of political struggle. Hence the UK government in the 2015 election gained less than 25% support of the adult electorate,[22] but can enforce laws that dictate how 100% of the electorate should behave. We shall see in Chapter 6 how elections are manipulated to give dominance to one sub-group over another. In this way, a party in power, by the will of a minority of the population, determines what laws and regulations are passed, and influences how all of them are enforced. Public hysteria, encouraged by the media and the 24-hour news cycle, may drive the statute and enforcement agenda in ways that are difficult for even the wisest of legislators to resist.

All this creates a legislative overload that is often selected from and applied with an unbalanced, even arbitrarily chosen emphasis. Citizens whose way of life does not fit can feel victimised. Most people feel it is far safer to pretend to acquiesce in the status quo than risk seeking to understand those who do not.

Rules and agreements that divide nations
In international affairs, the implementation of rules and resolutions can be even more dependent upon the power balance between nations. The well-armed ones and their friends can ride roughshod over majority decisions. The sense of unfairness this engenders leads to non-cooperation, even terrorism. Desperation can drive the stakes so high that some are ready deliberately to sacrifice their lives. In 2016, suicide bombing is just one of the weapons on the shelves of the alienated.

When the strong impose their will on the weak, redress can harm the innocent even more than the guilty. Lack of an ethical foundation in international affairs leads to agreements and dictates being arbitrarily broken. The avoidance and manipulation of an ever-increasing number of agreements creates a chaotic world, where religions and nations hold on to their own positions, be they right or wrong. Tragically, the world falls apart each group and nation knowing just what is needed to put things right, but being unable to trust the fairness and honesty of the others.

Societies and international relations dominated by rules, as most are in the twenty-first century, become neurotic maelstroms of misunderstanding. At best, they are like a bad-tempered sporting competition of winners and losers, determined by who is best at bending the rules to their advantage, or dominating by superior might. At worst, rules divide groups against each other, often in savagely intolerant ways. The experience of coloured races in the US southern states, or South Africa under apartheid; homosexuals in Russia; Jews in the Warsaw ghetto; or Palestinians in Gaza. At best, uneasy sub-groups grudgingly co-exist separately, resentful toward each other in an uneasy, non-cooperative peace.

If not to the above extremes, the tendencies to be separated by rules that only some accept exist in all societies. The extent to which this is so measures the extent to which those societies are dysfunctional. For rules to benefit, rather than injure society, they must appear to be fair and acceptable to as many people as possible.

If they are not founded upon an ethical wish to do the right thing and express universal respect, rules will always be used by the unscrupulous to control others. Then the well-behaved are exploited by cheaters, until they have put up with too much and decide 'So we will exploit them too'.[23]

Principles that could unite us

For millennia, enlightened teachers have told us not to judge and divide people like this, but to welcome them into an ever-widening community. Such understandings lie at the heart of most religions and humane philosophies; although not always in the churches into which the teachings have become institutionalised. Christ's Sermon on the Mount, Muhammad's practise of hospitality, Buddhist bodhicitta, nineteenth-century philanthropy, socialist idealism, a doctor's duty of care: these are just a few examples of a common core of idealistic respect for differences and the need for care between ourselves and others. When practised by societies, all of them lead to a sustainable way of life. We need to take narrow attachment to the trappings of our belief system[24] out of the equation. The last five chapters of this book seek to establish such idealism at the centre of an efficient free world economy.

To do this, we first need to understand errors in the key areas that cause our global disorder. These are described in Chapters 4 to 7. On the way to this understanding, astrocycles, whether explicitly mentioned or not, will play an important diagnostic role, offering insight into what drives events and the human decisions that influence them.

Using astrology to understand what seems to divide us
Because most of us lack sufficient saintliness to see into the hearts and minds of strangers without being destructively judgemental, we need an objective tool like astrology.

To suggest that astrology might have a useful role to play in this may amaze many people at first, but not if it is fully considered. We have seen that various human and animal perspectives of reality coexist in one Universe amidst the immensely contrasting cosmic forces of planets and their satellites, stars, galaxies, black holes, dark matter. Vast forces large and small, strong and weak, tolerate each other, because tolerance is unavoidable if we wish to survive. When an arrogant person or force tries to destroy an opposing person or force, the opposition always finds a way to neutralise any hope of total dominance by the other side. However the power play ebbs and flows, in the end, either both sides are destroyed, or both find and accept wise ways to accommodate each other. Like the planets, both find that the best way is to orbit around each other.

Because we live on the Earth we are subject to its conditions. Some of these are gross and obvious: air, sun, water, the ground we walk upon, the homes we live in and so on. Others are more subtle and difficult to see: electrical, chemical and biological processes. The power of computer technology administers our personal and commercial lives, even to the point where by attuning to satellites, aeroplanes and motor cars can drive themselves.

Before the increasing dominance of mechanics over our environment developed during the past 300 years, astrology was part of the decision-making process; used discreetly it still is today. Its cycles can be used to time actions. They repeat in regular patterns, but combine in virtually unique ways for each moment and each person. So, astro-cycles describe and explain the pattern of changing moods that drive events, but leave us free to make informed decisions. Because they cut across established religious and social assumptions of 'absolute truth', they help us put the assumed mores of societies and their rules in perspective. Because they describe the change that is happening, they help us to accept and use it effectively; we cease to be the victims of change. By knowing the background causes of an individual's nature and his specific actions, we can come to understand, respect and even love his assumptions and what he does. We are no longer inclined to reject them out of hand.

You can test this for yourself. *The Secret Language of Astrology*[25] offers an amazing range of concepts and tools, with which to understand relationships between individuals and with their societies. Astrological understanding reveals ways to get on with and grow with each other, while having differing views and ways of acting. It can be a great help in making friends and influencing people for the better.

Understanding astro-cycles puts another slant on the notion of time travel. Sci-fi enthusiasts have fantasised from Einstein's theories that it is possible to visit the past and the future physically. Whether his theory makes this possible or not,[26] by helping us empathise with other people and cultures, astrology offers the ability to see the past and future, to experience and feel its nature and what happened to the people, as if we were there.

Chapter 10 includes an astrologically-informed description of an ongoing global tragedy that touches very many people in different ways: as participants, protagonists, victims, innocent bystanders and concerned observers. Informing our experiences with astrology deepens our understanding of what those involved have and are going through. It may help us to seek and find wiser decisions to avert further tragedy.

Knowing the astro-cycles can help us understand issues closer to home. Family relations may have been caused by conflicting generational perspectives, which can be understood by comparing the longer cycles of the outer planets. *The Secret Language of Astrology* has all the tools to take a detailed look at the very different individual characteristics of yourself and those around you. Did the astro-cycles at a difficult moment of time make it more likely we would misunderstand, and behave impatiently? Could it be that someone we have fallen out with is as sad and desperate to put it right as us, but too frightened to take the first step? What is the best way to reconcile with a person like that? Why am I attracted to or alienated by that person, or that 'sort' of people? What astro-indicator can tell me whether the strong experience I have just had with someone is likely to last or fade? How long should I give it to be sure?

The unifying good heart that sets us free

There is just one Universe, but each person, family, group, society, nation, religion and culture sees it differently, and then sets rules that seek to make it their way. Rules to defend our separate ways lead to iron walls and fierce defensive weapons to keep out what appear to be baying groups intent on our destruction. Think again! See that all other beings are seeking safety, respect and happiness just as we do.

The flow of our lives does not have to be governed by the basest kind of knee-jerk reactions to the cycles of the heavens. By knowing and understanding the cycles, we can hold back and direct thoughts, words and actions in more beneficial directions. To do this, our insights and decisions must be grounded on open, accepted principles, not just confining ourselves self-interestedly to the mastery of those rules that suit our cause. Our intentions must be rooted in uncompromising kindness toward everyone.

Putting our minds into the experience of the society and history of others, taking refuge in the golden principle of care for each other, is the only way to resolve this. We can free all our fears, if we put aside posturing positions and instead talk to people under the banner of regret and recompense for wrongs done.

Rules and selectively implemented agreements cannot defend us. They merely *promise* freedom, while enslaving us in worlds and experiences we never wanted. Only the unifying good heart within us all can set us free.

Chapter 4
The Problem with Today's Science and Education

At the beginning of the twentieth century it was hoped, even expected, that religious and cultural conflicts between groups and nations would be corrected by the rational methods and discoveries of modern science. These would bring people together. All cultures would benefit from discoveries that eased the practical burdens of everyday life and ensured prosperity, without slavery, for everyone.

Less than two decades into that new century, the new technology's darker potential was unleashed in World War One, to slaughter millions of innocent people. The struggle to restrain the genie of global destruction in a protective bottle, amidst rapid advances in weapons development, overwhelmed the rest of the twentieth century and continues to this day.

Yet it is a popular assumption, encouraged by many twenty-first century opinion-leading scientists and their supporters, that their 'culture-free' methodology should dominate contemporary assumptions of reality; even though this methodology has no capacity to control what is done with what is discovered.

The benefits of modern science
Skilful tests, discoveries and reliable adaptations have enabled unstoppable improvements and greater control over our lives. The industry of millions of brilliant scientists has led to achievements of which everyone in our times should be justly proud. Working with an exact conscientious commitment that cuts through simplistic assumptions and superstitions, they have cleansed our world of many errors and opened amazing new possibilities.

The evidence of the rapid change is everywhere: on and under the ground, to the depths of the ocean, in the air, in space, in our ability to see far into what we claim to be 'the entire Universe' and 'the beginning of time itself'. For a modest fee, millions can fly around the globe, or stay where they are and make intimate virtual contacts across vast distances in mere moments of time. We can move mountains, build high into the sky and extract resources from deep down in the ground. We can change the nature of beings; we are even beginning to create life itself. Communication systems make organisations global, life is becoming increasingly uniform wherever you are in the world, and events can be beamed and known by everyone in an instant.

The problems of modern science
Amazing medical discoveries to defend against and cure disease and birth defects are lengthening life expectancy and its quality. We enjoy extra years that were just not available to most of our predecessors. Yet these medical benefits raise issues that are typical of many other aspects of our modern love affair with scientific advance and the statistical trials that underpin it.

The ingenious research, chemical power and mass statistical studies of allopathic medicine make what seem like miracle cures possible, but the very power of their efficacy comes with dangers. Over reliance on and incompetent use of antibiotics has led to the emergence of resistant bacteria. Over use in humans, as well as animals that humans eat, can weaken the immune system's ability to develop its own defences. Steroids are another miracle cure that seems to rejuvenate but has serious side-effects if over-used. Many ask if we are becoming too dependent on immunisation. Will giving the right dose to everyone eradicate the disease, just like that? While the benefits of these powerful cures and defences cannot be denied, none come without side effects. Rigorous testing always shows that they will not work on some people and indeed may do them serious harm. A sensitive minority suggest more reliance should be on *individual* inborn immunity. Maybe developments in individual genetic mapping will assist proper targeting. In time, the full astrological chart may well be used to enhance such targeting.

Sadly, at present, mainstream defensive attacks against alternatives dominate the debate. The argument over whether immunisation leads to autism is frenetic on both sides. In many other medical problems, subtle holistic alternatives, some used for thousands of years, giving steady but not dramatic benefits, are condemned as no better than placebos, or even 'harmful quackery'. Australian parents are denied child care benefits if they fail to have their children immunised; authorities are considering making it a legal requirement. The vast profits made by the commercial drug companies that develop and then market allopathic remedies to the medical professionals add further complexity.

How statistics can be counter productive
At the heart of these problems is the way modern science works. If statistics say a certain procedure has much better likelihood of success, although there are risks, then we would expect our doctor to advise us to have the treatment. However, should he go one step further and insist the treatment be legally enforced for children, if a parent resists, or even for all of us? What about the minority, for whom the treatment could be harmful, even lethal? There is usually another pill to compensate, and maybe a third or fourth to compensate for those. Being treated by such powerful medicines, patients lose the capacity to monitor what is happening to their bodies and become increasingly dependent upon their physician.

Individual patients should be fully informed, so they have the capacity to monitor and become the arbiter of decisions about their health. Alternative methods should not be dismissed, because simplistic statistical analysis is too gross to test treatments that are designed for individual circumstances. When modern science forces us to 'trust the experts' to make the right decisions regarding our health and other areas of our life, it takes away our individual freedom to know and decide for ourselves. In doing so, it not only disrespects and disempowers the citizens; it disempowers itself, by confining the progress to new discovery along ever narrower, linear, mechanical lines. Surely, knowing and being right about ourselves and our needs is the most valuable, life-saving insight anyone can have!

Medical science that moves towards denying individuals that right should be examined very carefully. We welcome powerful treatments, devised by skilful research and thoroughly tested on thousands of people. However, these should be avoided for minor illnesses and only prescribed after a sensitive interaction with the patient, to ensure they are appropriate. To allow statistical findings alone to rule patient diagnosis endangers the minority for whom the treatment is unsuited. If there were no other ways in our busy, underfunded health service, the minority may have to accept this harsh reality, but there are.

This said, to acquiesce in arbitrary claims that untested treatments should replace generally accepted ones could expose patients to unnecessary illness and death. Although often presented this way by mainstream medicine, the choice is not that extreme. Some complementary medicine techniques are older than Hippocrates. They put interaction with the patient at the centre and offer subtle treatments, designed to move him or her in a healing direction. While the time spent with the patient is valuable in all circumstances, obviously subtle treatments will rarely be effective in dire conditions. Complementary medicine approaches and treatments should be just that. When used to complement, they can fill a major gap in mainstream medicine; help it avoid dangerous over-prescribing and over-intervention. Together, both approaches could empower the patient in a truly ancient and modern holistic health service. Unfortunately, too few people in modern allopathic medicine accept such a balance. Many prefer to mock in demonstrations outside homeopathic clinics and start campaigns to deny funding. Even if their disputed claims that alternative treatments do not have testable dramatic good or bad effects were true, this would not mean they cannot have any effect at all. To claim so would fly in the face of patient experience, including the British royal family.[27]

Not only in medicine, but so many areas of our lives, modern science tends to insist on mechanical tests, not suited to the phenomena under study, before even considering approaches designed to educate individual choice and responsibility. Is the blind acceptance by more and more cultures of the exclusivity of this brave new world knowledge really the only way? Is such a rigid view the only way towards a healthier, more exciting and richer world for everyone? To answer this, we must consider the nature of science as it is commonly understood and practised today.

Is reductionist science able to correct *all* our limitations and answer *all* our social needs? If not, should we give it the authority we do?

The benefits and shortcomings of reductionist science

Reductionist scientific methodology believes that by looking at its individual constituents, we can understand a whole process. Even the complex and interacting physical processes of the human brain can be researched and understood by describing underlying chemical reactions that explain intelligence, emotion and human behaviour.

Many scientists question this. They say groups of people are too unpredictable to describe by formulas, based on a mass of individual observations. Turbulence, weather patterns and even the behaviour of crowds are difficult to explain by scientific reductionism. Isolating one phenomenon and studying it often changes its behaviour. Measuring both the position and speed of an electron is uncertain, because measuring one affects the other.

In genetics, while each amino acid of a protein can be coded on the DNA strand (reductionist) the overwhelming sequence of DNA provides endless 'structure' with its twisting, coiling and highly complex interaction it is, although, seemingly random. It has vital control functions which might never be explained by reductionist theory. Here the sum is certainly greater than its parts. This predicament in genetics is remarkably akin to that of astro-cycles, where the positions of and relationships between planets, with their associated keywords, are easy to know exactly, but the integrated meaning, much more multifaceted and general. Research marrying the language of these two great modern and ancient systems of knowledge should not be dismissed as arbitrarily as it is.

For thousands of years, philosophers have taught that the existence of things is dependent upon causes. When causes cease, so do the objects, ideas and experiences dependent upon them. Everything is subject to change and there are rules by which change occurs. Hence, while the modern view of 'scientific method' is invaluable in explaining and adapting our experiences, it cannot give absolute answers for all time. By its very conceptual nature, its findings are always limited to its research tools, design methods and, crucially, what it seeks to discover.

The instrument we use to observe and measure defines what we see: the tele- or microscope, heat, X-ray, night vision, normal photo, Nano vision, the hammer and the scalpel give us very different perspectives and capacities. What is hot or cold depends upon the temperature of the observer. Does red wine assist or harm our health, to what extent, in what kinds of people? Empirical discoveries through observation and statistical comparison are endless and often contradictory. Myriad scientific facts become like a vast macro-market for us to meander through, selecting those that 'suit our fancy'.

Depending upon what is in our self-interest, we can select facts (or various reasons) for or against, or even to deny the very existence of global warming. The efficacy of medicines depends upon the latest research and the questions we ask about them; which often suggests the need for further research. While the constant debate surrounding scientific discovery enhances our understanding and opportunities to change our world, its 'certainties' are subject to constant refinement and change. For this reason, science, as we know it today, cannot be the final arbiter of the decisions we make. Such a claim would cross a Rubicon; making it a belief system, akin to and not necessarily greater or truer than, any other belief system.

Clarifying the limits of reductionist science

Most scientists would insist that to say they make such a claim is 'rubbish'; the very opposite of the intrinsic nature and intention of their work. Yet, led on by the media and politicians who hide behind 'expert advice', majorities in many societies do act as if scientific research is the only way to truth. Such mindsets are buoyed up with high-profile campaigns by vocal secular scientists. Methods they claim to be dangerously outside, or irrelevant to, mainstream research are denied voice and resources.

Such attitudes are driven by an unquestioned assumption that the very approach underpinning their work is sacrosanct. There is no other way than their 'scientific method' to test and know. Yet is not the first principle of science to challenge to the very core all assumptions, and especially the method itself? It is an ironic paradox that the freedom of knowing through objective enquiry, developed from the Renaissance through the Enlightenment, is today in danger of becoming the very fundamentalist opposite of its intrinsic nature.

It is vital to move back from this profoundly dangerous tendency to see reductionist science as the final arbiter in major decisions. For it is at its weakest when considering those very human areas of desire and emotion that drive decision-making. Machines may map the electronic and chemical processes of the brain. We may be able to develop chemicals and interventions that change, correct, even control, human behaviour, but we are only monitoring and containing the external manifestation. Something more is inside that the scientist can only guess at. A prison guard can lock up and restrain the movements of an inmate, even make him scream in pain. Yet without reaching the heart of the prisoner's motivation, he will only terrorise, not change his unshakeable inner truth. Indeed, his unkind actions may well reinforce the opposite of what he seeks.

However advanced our knowledge of human technology becomes, key questions remain. How to decide what to do with what we know and who do we appoint to adjudicate? 'On what basis would we control the controller?' Could we improve on Aldous Huxley's Brave New World, where mechanical science takes all responsibility for procreation? Test tube foetuses are created in five clear categories, suited to their designated social roles from Alpha (governing) to Epsilon (unskilled workers). In this world, everyone knows their place. Entertainment is spectacularly commercialised. Sexual experience is entirely recreational and chemically created. Nothing is left to chance in a static and intrinsically heartless society. Is this all we want?

At present, we leave this question unanswered, because reductionist science has no method to assess how we choose our leaders and the decisions they make. Culture-free mechanical scientists create methods and machines that affect just about every area of our lives, but then awkwardly say it is for the humane sciences to help us decide whether, when and how to use them.

Yet, to a considerable extent these sciences, such as economics, politics, sociology and psychology have the same limitations. Many of their studies focus on quantitative statistical research and so offer the same kind of non-judgemental descriptive information as the mechanical sciences. Knowing how many people in social classes, places or sexes display behaviour patterns can be used to exploit, harm or help.

It is only when the humane sciences move into descriptive qualitative research that they can give us the experience of the intentions, actions and consequences of human behaviour. However anecdotal, a carefully designed combination of opinions and motivations of people acting in various roles can inform the life blood that judges and decides. That a behaviour pattern is associated with chemical or electrical changes in the brain may explain or even be used to justify behaviour. Knowing outcomes from support group activities can educate individuals to work with and make positive use of such tendencies. This is a much better way to go.

The danger of relying on reductionist science
In two contradictory ways, the amorality of reductionist science serves the policies of the politicians and the interests of the business people who rule our lives. On the one hand, the business and political interests select scientific findings that justify their desire-based actions. On the other hand, should things go wrong, they scapegoat the scientists and their findings; use them as an excuse to hide behind.

Political decisions are based on self- and sub-group interests, which are mainly determined by loyalties driven by emotion: pride, greed, jealousy and anger. Most world leaders today have a fragmentary grasp of, or interest in, objective, ethical considerations. What moral training they have tends to be from traditional religious backgrounds. Many of these were institutionalised to sustain cultural prejudice at times when the world was less interconnected.

Here lies the core cause of the race to global destruction. We live in a world that is developing ever more powerful methods of control over our material environment, but is ruled by adolescent decision-making. We can compare today's world to a luxury home, left for the weekend by indulgent parents for their sixteen-year-old children 'to invite a few friends round'.

Is there a better way to develop an ethical foundation in our relationships and business dealings? Is there something we can draw from the past? It seems unlikely! Values in the past were even more institutionalised in the service of narrow self-interest than today. Fortunately, they did not have the weapons! Francisco Pizarro could put tens of thousands of Incas to the sword, but not sit at home threatening distant lands with drones. Adolf Hitler could gas millions of Jews, but not obliterate Israel with a few nuclear weapons.

Spiritual values can contain misuse of scientific discovery
Within each culture's belief system, far deeper and more important than the megalomaniacal attempts by those in power to marshal the people to hate and destroy 'infidels' and 'pagan blasphemers', lies a pure heart of tolerance and kindness towards all. This sublime, pure, generous heart, deep within all religions, struggles to sustain itself and be heard. From this struggle emanates the greatest mythology, children's tales, literature, art, philosophy and music, which show something wonderful and magical can live in us, hearten and bring us together.

Some secular scientists side line such areas of experience, citing how belief and superstition are used to marshal populations against each other. Talking this way dangerously misses the point. The cause of such horrors is not symbolic stories or spiritual idealism, but the way both are usurped by the very same self-interest-driven institutionalised misuse that misappropriates today's science. To fix on narrow certainty is not at all like the youthful open-minded spirit of enquiry of modern science's Enlightenment founders. Too many of today's scientists grudgingly accept art and culture as recreational activities, to be studied as phenomena, otherwise outside the scope of the decision-making process.

With inconsistent illogicality, today's science ignores the right of consideration to the very tools of ethical understanding that it does not itself have. Snow White and that gorgeous red, but poisoned, apple; Frodo's struggle with Gollum over the temptation of the ring; the dangers of following the Pied Piper; that Star Wars 'force' that will always be with us, are a few of the thousands of images we should have in our minds when deciding on political leaders, or what to do with certain scientific discoveries.

The teachings of great religious leaders have a common core, leading to the same conclusions in amazingly different ways. These cores should be cherished and integrated together into universal understanding, placed at the key centre of education. Whether fairy stories are true or believed is unimportant, what they symbolise is what counts. They train the mind to see possibility and wonder in everything, never to dismiss, always to seek promise, to love all creation. They enshrine the magic that grows from looking for the best in others, beyond obvious initial judgements. Such ways of thinking fuel the originality that is the driving force behind great scientific discoveries. Without it, Darwin was unlikely to have had the courage to undertake studies that led to him turning away from the accepted Creationist beliefs of his time. By telling fairy tales to our children, we teach them our values and caution them against self-indulgent temptation.

Every culture has a rich tradition of myth and legend. It is how the Greeks explored and advised on every aspect of psychology, relationships and emotion. Their images of parent-child relationships we still use today; explored through the travails of Odysseus, his tragic homecoming, Oedipus's relationship with his parents, the compassion of Prometheus, and, especially suited for reductionist scientists, Icarus! Myths, folk rhymes, tales and literature lie at the heart of our culture, its words, music and fine art. They are built into the way we speak and the names we give to things – even planets and other heavenly bodies. Throw out devotion, myth and fantasy and you throw out love and intimacy. You throw out originality, the right to challenge reason in the quest to discover a higher reason.

Vitally, you throw out the tools of the very process that may through example, discussion and reflection lead to principles that wisely contain and direct the way we use our new, ever more powerful scientific knowledge.

The transitory history of 'absolute truth'

So, systems of knowledge should be regarded as 'horses for courses'. If you want to build a house that will last, you will follow the advice of a good structural engineer, but not necessarily his political opinions. The best way to decide who or what to trust is through our own objective wisdom and sensitivity. With these most of us can discern the rigour of other people's principles. Bringing in astro-cycles can further objectify our judgement. It can allow even clearer insights to shine through, while putting conventional assumptions in perspective.

In common with nearly all cultures for thousands of years, we have a strong subconscious tendency to assume our contemporary society has reached the overriding endgame to date in the pursuit of truth. We have transcended the ignorance of our forebears. There may be a lot more things to learn, but our method to assess and learn them is fixed and will not change.

The lesson of history is that such assumptions never turn out to be so. The history of knowledge shows that yesterday's refreshing new view of reality, the transformation of the Dark Ages by Christianity perhaps, becomes today's 'indisputable' and increasingly oppressive orthodoxy, the nature of the fifteenth-century Roman Catholic Church before the Reformation. Society transforms like this from generation to generation, age to age. Each time it assumes itself to be the final, indisputable custodian of absolute truth, only to be shown to be incomplete and wrong. Crucially, the more certain and insistent sub-groups, or even whole periods in history, are about the absolute nature of *their* truth, the nearer that truth is to its endgame nemesis.

Our time is no different to any other. Fortunately, or unfortunately, depending upon how you feel about it (especially for modern reductionism), we are living at a time of fundamental social transformation. Wise thinkers from many disciplines are talking about this. Those who use astrology point out that the underlying cycles of the outer planets, especially Pluto, make this clear.

Pluto's cycle indicates the removal of past dysfunctional attitudes and the rebirth of something new and better in its place. The nature of the transformation is indicated by its zodiac sign. Its sign positions over the past one hundred years show this. In Cancer 1912-39 it meant the death and transformation of political and individual family structures; in Leo 1937-56 death and transformation through megalomania; when it joined with Uranus in Virgo 1956-71 the critical upheaval of the past; in Libra 1971-83 the death and transformation of relationships; in Scorpio 1983-95 death and transformation of sexuality; in Sagittarius 1995-2008 the death and transformation through travel and globalisation. Since 2008, it has been in Capricorn, indicating death and transformation of the planet's structure, systems and transactions; a struggle for control over these between individuals and the state.

Its 246-year cycle means it was previously in Capricorn in the early sixteenth century. The then dominant Roman Catholic Church's 'absolute truth', coming from divine dictate, was challenged, along with the notion of a God-focused geocentric Universe. From out of the brutal mist of horrendous centuries-long religious conflict emerged a rational view of man. His research studies were largely to replace deistic institutions, as the observer and arbiter of reality. When next in Capricorn in the latter part of the eighteenth century, it marked the first stage of failure in absolute rule by aristocracy and the Divine Right of Kings. Rule by right of birth faced a struggle for 'the rights of man'. Such views built to the American and French Revolutions and the ensuing campaigns for individual rights and democracy in the centuries that followed.

Pluto in Capricorn again (2008-24) is a seeding time of the next stage in the process. We are at the beginning of the end of rule determined by the right of acquired power, based on the pursuit of possessions, position and symbolic knowledge. Scandals have led to public distrust of just about every institution of social control: politicians, police, bankers, journalists, even medical professionals. When not seduced by it, we are learning ways to challenge the absolute power of greed, ignorance, even hatred, in the running of our institutions. Increasingly, individuals will now demand the right to know, decide and organise their own lives. In previous Pluto-in-Capricorn cycles we have freed ourselves from oppressive rule over our very soul. We have established the right to form and practise our own beliefs. Then we challenged hereditary authority and created new institutions and businesses, where we could be seen, act and organise as equals. Now, in the third cycle, we are developing the power to enjoy equal opportunities to shape our *individual* lives for good or ill and make society the sum total of all of us, however powerful the authorities who are against this happening.

As in the two previous times, Pluto in Capricorn can empower the oppressors even more strongly than those seeking liberation. The consequences of inquisitions and religious wars still fester to this day. Five hundred years after the Reformation, religious absolutists continue to battle. The struggle for democracy is hardly won and its true nature little understood or accepted in most contemporary societies.

The Enlightenment's shortcomings and those of the eighteenth- and nineteenth-century industrialisation that followed can be seen in the ever-expanding international corporations that dominate our lives today. Much scientific discovery has been hijacked and used for the mindless consumption of the Earth's resources. Government and commercial interests seek to dominate the Internet. Together at the heart of it all, these powerful institutions combine to control the educational means by which we initiate our young people.

Initiating the new generation in our modern world

The initiation of new generations is the key adult responsibility in human and most animal societies. Birds prepare comfortable, safe nests and work ceaselessly to feed their young, until they are ready to fly freely with the flock. They seem to know when to push them into independence.

In traditional human societies, ornate initiation ceremonies mark the passage from adolescence to adulthood. In more complex human cultures, formal education fulfils this function. The actual time that a child is ready to leave the close care of its parents and enter an educational institution is not commonly agreed upon. However, in today's commercially competitive world, where both parents work, ways of freeing day-to-day parental responsibility are available at an ever-younger age. Nursery education from three or four years is becoming standard in most developed societies; even earlier if the job is important enough to afford a minder. A mother returning to work three months after a child's birth is becoming less rare.

This means that not only the imparting of educational knowledge but also the development of the social experience and attitudes of vulnerable young minds is given over to strangers. Except in informal baby-minder arrangements, these strangers are registered and supervised by the state. The way the state fulfils this responsibility will depend upon the social attitudes and expert advice accepted by those in power. Our elected politicians nowadays make central decisions regarding the correct training and standards to be achieved, even by pre-school children. Carers and teachers of our children, however warm and kindly devoted, are becoming dictated to by narrow academic goals over which parents have no control. Indeed, because they are without proper academic training, do parents have the right to any opinion at all?

In our advanced modern world, the education of children, and so the initiation of our people into adulthood, is controlled by a dominant assumed truth. Its systems of initiation and enforcement are decided by 'highly-qualified' experts and complex regulations that guide and protect their every decision. This knowledge is financed by, and is the reinforcing supporter of, the commercial and political forces in power. So, carers and teachers are left powerless, needing to 'keep to the guidelines'. From three years old, the academic emphasis for a child is a systematic initiation into the assumed truths of the commercial and political elite. Young minds are at the mercy of those mutually and inextricably linked to a greed-driven political world view.

We are educating our children in the secular faith

Atheists and extreme reductionist scientists make much of the dangers of distorting even grooming vulnerable young minds in faith schools. They point to those established by Islamic, Jewish, Christian and other religious communities. Such concern is based on a false premise: the assumption that believing in no God (or even believing in the absolute reliability of scientific methods and the kind of 'rational' society that leads to) is anything more than just another belief system. All schools are faith schools and, make no mistake about it, *conventional secular education is our dominant faith school system*; no more, no less!

Reductionist science may be fundamental to understanding the modern world, but to allow its view of reality to have absolute priority goes too far. This turns it into a belief system. Then, by peddling its relative reality as the vital, life-saving fashion of our time, it dangerously distorts education.

For, the intrinsic nature of scientific understanding has changed over the years – not always making linear progress. The Greeks were wiser than the Romans, who were wiser than most of the barbarians that followed. We rediscovered much of the best of both classical cultures and have made great new advances over the last 300 years. Yet, as we have seen, the 'scientific method' many take refuge in today is just not equipped to describe and understand everything. The supposed ultimate point it takes us to (e.g. the nineteenth-century atom, now, the twenty-first century Hadron awareness) turns out to be just a gateway to vast new worlds to investigate; now with new tetra quark matter.[28]

Wise people looking back at us from the future will wonder with amazement if we continue to ignore so much of our esoteric and philosophical heritage. Our descendants may well turn upside down what contemporary scientists assert as indisputable. Today's Darwinists wonder at the limitations of their nineteenth-century predecessors, but are not many of today's Darwinists the same prejudiced people-types as Darwin's nineteenth-century Creationist detractors?

Yet, despite all these reservations to win 'The Global Economic Race', we are subjecting our children to a quantitative reductionist mechanical view of reality. Curricula are increasingly distorted to focus on the attainment and testing of number and language skills, as a means of successful competition against other pupils and economies. Schools' curricula increasingly adopt this emphasis, while downgrading art, music, literature and social understanding as less important. This will feed through to university studies and hence radically change the very cultural knowledge nature of our society.

Methods, such as astrology,[29] that aim to unify our understanding of and behaviour toward each other are refused consideration. Objects, and methods to attain them, become more important than the responsibility that should come from having them. Stardom is more greatly sought after than the art of performance. Power over others and the natural environment is more valued than knowing and enjoying them. Winners receive the accolades, everyone else the pickings. In such a world, knowledge is functional rather than appreciated and prized for itself.

Education for a happy world
The current way we educate our children into an acquisitive secular faith does not reflect how we are, or what we are naturally comfortable with. Nearly all parents seek happiness for their children above everything else. Indeed, at heart, all fellow humans seek happiness and would hope other people have the same experience. Campaigns to raise money for those in need through hardship or disaster are remarkably well supported. Yet, because we do not understand and address the root cause of most inequality and suffering, we feel overwhelmed. We feel invaded by the constant demand of others' needs. This gets in the way and dissatisfies our lives.

Focusing on material possession and desires has been the curse and cause of conflict between people and peoples from the beginning of time. Shortage and hardship is used to justify the struggle to survive. Leaders manipulate hope to drive us toward the glory of conquest. Today's science gives humanity ever greater control and enabled many more of us to survive. Great new communication technology enables us to know and be involved in cultures all over the world. We need an educational system that prepares our children for this. It should not shut out the strange for fear it will threaten, but should meet, welcome and incorporate new knowledge to enrich everyone's lives. We need an education that is not just about making and marketing, but about being, enjoying, expanding and understanding. We need not an unholy alliance of science and business that gives accolades to the most profitable at the expense of everyone else. We do not need an educational system that prepares our children with false 'promises' of success. We need education for an economy that recognises, fairly administers, and so offers hope for everyone.

Such an education will not trim itself down in a futile chase after the learning hot-houses of emerging economies. Why are we desperately rushing to catch up with what we have already achieved, weighed in the balance and found wanting? Our education will instead focus on a core of deep principle and of fair give and take. These are the key tools to create a world that everyone can enjoy together. It will make realistic attempts to understand and address injustice, wherever it is, however long-term its causes and difficult it may be to resolve. It will transcend the moral and economic incompetence of our contemporary 'me first' social organisation. It is the responsibility of the more fortunate, richer societies to take the lead in the discovery and glory of this new education.

The principle-based education we need will draw on a broad understanding of the art and wisdom of many world cultures and times. By comparing notes it will see and show the common decency that lies at the heart of creation. Such an education will always be a work in progress, always open to new knowledge and ways of seeing and acting. For, what binds us together in happy lives is the principled motivation behind our quest to care for others and our world. All other knowledge should be put in its place to serve this end.

This is the way to initiate all our children into a worthy world.

Chapter 5 - The Problem with Society

What a society believes about itself determines how its people experience their lives within it; but how and by whom are these beliefs decided?

From earliest times, when hunter-gatherers grouped, dominant individuals' understandings of the nature of things would be listened to and followed. Because this influence could control their society's knowledge base, the self-interest of the most articulate speakers would decide the social guidelines.

In more complex societies, sub-groups develop specialist control over certain areas of knowledge and activity. Leaders within these groups have a special personal privilege to influence, even determine, social beliefs and the rules to enforce them. So, when talking about the beliefs of a society, it is crucial to consider how these beliefs are determined and administered. Who leads? Are beliefs the product of the people's aspirations and how they collectively see life and their place in the Universe, or a mere manipulated function of its leading members' self-interest?

Some potential leaders will be idealists, who seek to benefit all; even exceptional 'Wheel Turning Kings,[30] whose higher truth inspires and establishes ethical societies. Chapter 8 considers the Confucian value system's role in establishing such societies. At the other extreme, determined idealists may have sufficient revolutionary force to destroy the status quo, only to replace it with yet another system, dominated by their privileged group.

Most aspirants to leadership proclaim disconnected fragments of idealism, designed merely to inspire hope rather actually change or achieve anything. Calling themselves 'realists', these simplify and narrow the focus of belief to gain mastery for personal gain. The most successful of these will gather people on some 'great enterprise' to benefit their sub-group at the expense of everyone else.

Here comes danger. When exclusive belief combines with physical power, conflict between believers and non-believers is near to inevitable. 'Death to the non-believer', even in a literal sense, can be easily justified. Appetites whetted by success, the great conquerors throughout history destroyed their enemies in vast numbers and brought home booty. Then used the power of its wealth to create empires with scant regard for the suffering of those they conquered.

Warrior states and empires

For millennia, these underlying factors determined social structures in Babylon, Egypt, China, Mongolia, Persia, Greece, Rome and medieval Europe. Loyalty and service toward the leader or privileged sub-group was rewarded with goods and land. This created an aristocracy, supported by slaves, or the servitude of suppliant peasants. Skilful negotiations in business dealing enriched the merchant class. So, hierarchical structures emerged to serve the aims of the leader, be it the emperor, the king or all-important state. Religious beliefs became the institutionalised driving force that reinforced the state and brought people together in life or death struggles for what they held to be 'their way life'. From this came the Divine Right of secular kings to rule on behalf of God, whose messengers were the priests of the established churches. In feudal medieval Europe, the peasant population was beholden for land and protection to their lord and his squires. In return the Lord took a portion of peasants' produce for himself and used them as an army at his disposal.

Contemporary societies

So it remained until the fifteenth-sixteenth centuries. Then, change came subtly at first, with the coming of printing and publishing in the vernacular which led to the Protestant schism. Now intellectuals and even the ordinary people began to question religious teachings and the authority system sustained by them. In the eighteenth-nineteenth centuries, the expansion of enterprise and exploration, along with population movements due to industrialisation, accelerated human rights demands.[31]

For centuries, the unjust treatment of the common people had been an undercurrent, ready for a hook, by which to rise and rebel. It was given irresistible momentum by the social changes caused by the eroding of absolute feudal authority, as vast populations moved from the land. Yet, the aristocratic system held much of its ground into the early twentieth century, even expanding its presence into empires throughout the globe. It was only after two terrible World Wars that they it gave in to popular movements. Aristocracy was replaced by meritocracy.

While rule based on birth right had largely broken down by the mid twentieth century, this did not mean that ordinary citizens gained authority over their lives. Rather, control now passed to a meritocracy of expert position-holders, who claimed that only they had the expertise and sense of responsibility to rule on the people's behalf.

So, while the lives of ordinary people today seem more prosperous, and certainly less menial, the power structure has seen little real change. There are new ways to power and new kinds of people may hold it, but the relationship between the people and their rulers, the ability of a privileged minority to decide and control the majority's lives, has not substantially changed. What we think and do today is as much determined by those that hold the power and purse strings as it ever was.

The old estates may have been broken up, or converted into public or theme parks, but the gap between rich and poor continues to grow. Our way of life may not be controlled by position at birth, but is just as controlled by: the scientists and educators who determine what we know and should know about our world and ourselves; the economists, who determine how we should work and spend our rewards; the politicians and lawyers, who make, or fail to make and enforce the rules by which we live our lives; and their communicators who develop ingenious ways to tell us and our families what to think, want, have and do.

Cultural dictatorship by the 'meritocracy'

In this way, the control system by society's leaders today is more intrusive and absolute than the royal and aristocratic power dominance of earlier times. The peasant in his cottage may have been focused on loyalty to his noble master but, within their home and sub-group, families were masters of their own culture and destiny. Many feudal lords saw themselves as having a duty of care for their peasants.

In our times, life is more comfortable and indulgent, punishment less severe, we can even complain. However, those in charge are an amoral group who lack any tradition of what it is right to do, other than to consume and encourage others to do so by numbing sensitivity and intelligence.

The importance of this cannot be overemphasised. When millions of viewers involve themselves, take solace, even joy, in the lives of TV soap characters and hang upon celebrity personalities and opinions, the nature of society and its values is profoundly affected. More sinister is that these key formative influences in the recreational areas of people's lives are financed by businesses seeking to profit by encouraging and indulging consumers. Could there be a more telling indication of the derogatory way those who control the resources of society view those that use them? By careful research, minds are manipulated, bought and sold. So, money and power, not opinion, discussion and judgement, drive the way society is understood and politically organised.

Cynicism and disbelief in the good intentions of everyone and everything become accepted as the 'natural way' of the world; self-interested motivation the key to success. Acquiring the resources to succeed in an unprincipled exploitative world, when everyone who is anyone is in it for themselves, is all-important. 'If they do it, why should I not do the same?'

Egged on by the carrot that any one of us could build the same riches as Bill Gates, be as admired and famous as David Beckham, as loved as Catherine, Duchess of Cambridge, or as 'amusingly informed' as Stephen Fry, we continue to work harder. Would we not be guilty of envy to deny the winner the spoils? Accepting the status quo, the proletariat is emasculated by feeling just not good, wise or hard-working enough to be more than a failed aspirant on the road to success. When the few laud it over the many and organise society for their own benefit, society is profoundly weakened, narrowed and lacking in creativity. This leaves ordinary people unable to know their power and stand up for themselves.

Lacking a creative, alternative strategy, we are told to accept that the only way to be happy is to limit ourselves, our relationships and children to developing the best skills possible to 'win the global race'. Whether we can, or even want to, seems uncertain, but those in power and influence over us 'know best'.

Consequences of not playing the game

Chapter 6 will show how those disengaging from or disagreeing with the race are marginalised and even attacked by popular politicians and are poorly reported, usually misreported, in the established media. The cynical ways this is done are skilfully designed to make the very actions of those rejecting the system seem to support the need for its existence!

Rather like the 'savages' in Aldous Huxley's *Brave New World*, those refusing to join the race chose to survive as best they can in their 'left behind' world. Some may resort to crime. Most survive by mirroring the ways of society's rich

The Problem with Society

and privileged few; those business leaders, who ignore principles and twist the rules for personal advantage. At the same time, they force those rules on the people who serve their needs, canonising them as 'hard-working families', while depressing their wages and cutting services!

Learning from the ways of the rich, some of those at the other end of the social structure twist the rules of the welfare system to make it a basic source of income, often supplemented with odd jobs in the black economy. In what is sometimes referred to in the UK as 'sink estates', cultures of dependency have developed that span several generations. Their radically different culture, outside the pressures of the global race, is often castigated. Their existence is used by those in power as a stick to beat down not just them, but everyone who cannot live properly without welfare support.

Little research is done and cited as to what proportion this group makes up of the whole welfare budget. In fact, most funds go to those it was designed to help: the genuinely disabled and people fallen on hard times in severe and desperate need. Furthermore, a considerable amount of the welfare budget covers part-time or low-wage workers. Here, by subsidising wages through tax credits, the government is supporting the employers and their shareholders rather than their workers.

Those who proactively question and challenge the system are skilfully manipulated to be seen as its lunatic, even dangerous fringes. It is said that too much action on global warming or campaigns citing the dangers of nuclear power generation and fracking will lead to everyone paying very high power bills; even to the lights going out.

When world business and political leaders gather at costly extravaganzas (travel, accommodation and hospitality paid by their customers and citizens) to decide the nature and conditions of ordinary people's lives, protests are often put down by severe security. The struggles that ensue are shown in a way that suggests this is what it will be like 'if ever those kinds of people and their ideas are taken seriously'. So, the established system is clearly the only sane option! To reinforce this impression, the issues raised by the protesters are always reported in the most banal way. The media concentrate on who got through the barriers, violence, arrests, police behaviour and the like, not what the protests were about. No serious alternatives are discussed, only minor nuances of disagreement to the main thrust amidst the privileged group's empty grand promises.

The aristocraticisation of the proletariat
For all the faults of today's world, surely, we must accept that there is no better alternative? Surely it is true that 'One-person-one-vote democracy is the worst system of social organisation, except for all the others'!

Until the disintegration of the Soviet system during the 1989-92 outer-planetary opposition (Jupiter in Cancer to Saturn, Uranus and Neptune in Capricorn), various attempts to apply Marxist economic theory to social organisation argued that it offered better alternatives to the exploitative colonial capitalism described in Chapter 2. Indeed, for over 100 years, the struggle between the two clearly flawed economic philosophies dominated political argument.

Although colonial capitalism had reached its sell-by date and was ready for radical reform in the 1930s, the horrors of Neptune-in-Virgo fascism, and then the 1947-89 Cold War, triggered by the Saturn-Pluto conjunction in Leo, took over the agenda. Compared to the Soviet Politburo dictatorship, the system of western capitalist democracy, born out of European and then also American paternal colonialism, seemed like Utopia. So it was that, at the fall of the Berlin Wall in 1989, the triumph of capitalism was declared and Marxism consigned to the scrap heap of failed idealisms.

Looking back over the years since then and the state of economic and political relationships today, it may seem that this 1989 declaration was as facile and premature as was George W Bush's 2003 'Mission Accomplished' speech. Now knowing what happened in Russia after the Soviet collapse and the failings of our current western system, we should look again at why Marxism failed. When we do, it opens the door to reveal how to put right our modern world.

When writing *Das Kapital*, Marx was reacting to brutal exploitation of workers in the industrialisation of the early nineteenth-century. He demonised the social class system as its cause. Capitalist owners were by their very position the exploitative enemy of the working class, the bourgeoisie their middle-class apologists and functionaries. To become an employer was to become an exploiter; the foreman was the toddie scab servant of the employer, all workers were the downtrodden victims of the system. Only when this system broke down under its own corrupt inadequacy and the workers became masters of 'the commanding heights of the economy' would a happy and just society be established.

Looked at not only in the context of those times, but many times since and in some of today's societies, it is undeniable that the privilege of social power corrupts and can lead to the oppression of others. This does not mean it must. Movements inspired by Marxism and socialism may not have created whole-country Utopias on Earth, but many have successfully led the way in the struggle for material social justice within societies.

We saw in Chapter 4 how scientific discovery and technological advances have enriched masses of ordinary people. Many seem to live as well today as did their aristocratic forebears. They can surf the web for the best foods to be delivered to their door and prepared by advanced machines with the click of a few buttons, while they watch a favourite artist on one of their many types of screens. How little different is this from the experience of a noble lord in the 'big house' pulling a cord and having what is needed brought to him during an evening musical soirée? So, we have the aristocraticisation of the proletariat, but do these ordinary people, or anyone else, experience our modern world as Utopia? Are they not more like our aristocratic forebears or nineteenth-century employers, caught up in their own world and needs; desensitised as to how it is to live without what they now feel is essential; ignorant about the world outside and the way their actions contribute towards its ills?

Here we come to the vital built-in failure in the Marxist analysis. If people's experiences are the product of their social position, when that social position changes we can expect them to take on the characteristics of their new social position. That mass groups of workers, certain races and tribes are dispossessed today does not mean they will behave with superior idealism when they have possessions tomorrow. Marxist analysis clearly revealed the shortcomings of the exploitative capitalist class system, but, lacking class-free spiritual and ethical principles, its resolution methods were essentially flawed. Marxism and socialism could do no better than push the capitalist system to aristocraticalise[32] the proletariat, to live in dissatisfied plenty in a dysfunctional world, without hope of a balanced middle way that could be constantly correcting injustice.

All kinds of better people can create better worlds

Indeed, with his dictum 'religion is the opium of the people' Marx slammed shut the open door to anything better. Certainly, the relationship between many established churches and their flock could be described as the dispensing of opiates. Yet the kind integrity at the heart of a genuine spiritual aspirant holds within it great ethical courage. With unshakeable principled power, the aspirant recognises what is needed and becomes devoted to the constant correction of injustice. In the nineteenth century, people from all walks of life came forward with brave hearts to urge major changes to rescue under-classes; bringing people out of penury, children and adults out of slavery.

Selfless empathy and the capacity to see beyond immediate danger makes any person from any class and group capable of facilitating such change, as long as the system they live under empowers them by allowing the right to know and hold opinions.

It is here that today's system of information and social control fails. Carefully choreographed opportunities[33] to give to the needy may reveal natural generosity in people's hearts. Unfortunately, they also let the masses off the hook of their root-cause responsibility for the suffering of the under-classes in today's world's, who slave to keep privileged sub-groups and countries in aristocratic ease. The economy may prosper by encouraging ever more consumption to satisfy such demand-based ease; but only if those enjoying the comfort do not question the system that provides it. So, as refugees and immigrants knock ever more insistently on the doors of Europe and the US, are we any more than indulged, impotent observers, going through the motions? Are not our lives reminiscent of those characters in Chekov's *The Cherry Orchard*, living in Tsarist Russia through its dwindling years?

It is this paradox of plenty that prevents ordinary western people opening their hearts to create a better world society for everyone. It will come when the intrinsic qualities in all people of all classes see through and transcend the assumptions of their system. The outer planet astro-cycles will not let us rest. They constantly mark the change in underlying social assumptions and trends. They nudge us away from resting on our laurels.

However unsettling this feels, welcome it. Every change makes us wiser and more able to master the way to freedom and real success.

Chapter 6
The Problem with the Media and Politics

The pervasive, insistent glue that integrates, justifies and so holds together the economic, legal, scientific, educational and political institutions of today's consumption-based authority system are the news, information, marketing and entertainment systems of the communications industry.

In the previous chapter, we saw how in the past ruling classes and religious institutions controlled the people by irresistible power, harsh punishment and fear of the afterlife, yet otherwise left them to live as they wished. Also, the quality of ordinary people's lives today appears to be more like the lives of aristocrats in earlier years: labour-saving devices, an amazing range of foods, nightly entertainment beamed into their homes, and the ability to communicate and travel more widely than ever before.

Despite all these comforts, today's control by the rich and famous over ordinary people is far more intrusive. The communications industry rules us by reaching into our minds to trap dispositions.

Channelling access to knowledge limits the confidence to form objective opinions. Today's authority system may have a friendly face, but it is far more insidious than authorities of old. It comes much closer, past the thresholds into the living rooms of our homes. As an unavoidable condition of access, deeply embedded into the entertainment comes the marketing of the special interests of the paymasters, along with cultural assumptions, backed up by opinion-creating 24-hour newscasts. This system takes over every individual soul, adopting the same role that religion fulfilled in previous times. By encouraging our tastes and interests, it cajoles us into the required actions that its experts and our leaders decide are best for us.

What's on the news?

The Ancient Greeks knew the potential of presenting archetypal, profound stories as mass extravaganzas. Great annual festivals brought people to experience captivating tragedy and comedy, based on archetypal mythology, handed down from ancient times. These stories reached so deeply into the heart of human nature that key classical characters and concepts remain built into modern psychology. Oedipus and Electra complexes, catharsis, nemesis, the terror of consequences, conscience, and unavoidable divine justice are at the very heart of dramatic tragedy in our own day. Greek drama was the grand spectacle of its day, like our modern world sports' events, but its insights were far deeper, advanced and permanent in impact than the transitory overnight 'booze-ups' that mark the winning of a sporting trophy in our own time.

Today, the various 24-hour TV news outlets and print media are the nearest we get to public catharsis: a disappearance or sad death, legal battle, natural disaster, a scandal, a fall from grace, a triumph (against all odds maybe) or a reunion. These things we share through the news, but, in their breadth, depth and insight, do they reach the cathartic impact found in Ancient Greek drama, or rather just titillate the surface of public interest?

Some real issues from courageous and principled reporters may be heard, touch hearts and genuinely inform the people. Indeed, much of this book's confirming background comes from journalists and editors with the courage to go to places, and to report leaks from whistle-blowers. Some of these risk everything, even their lives, to tell the world how resources are controlled and administered, and so shape what people can have and do.

However, the news selection and sanitised presentation, determined by the underlying culture-based assumptions of truth, held by the owners and their editors, mean that most news channels merely touch on the surface of the public soul. News windows of just a few days can mean that issues are soon forgotten. Channels, such as US's *Fox News* and Russia's RT network, contrive to stir emotion in prejudiced directions, outraging excessively. Most appear to be objective and sympathetic in their reporting, but the presentation is always from a narrow middle window of 'credibility'. Established 'expert' testament confirms the generally held view and often reinforces prejudice in less didactic ways. Often the news just distracts by creating fads to chase. The public is left powerless, with a jaundiced view of situations over which they have no control. Much easier to decide that the news has little, or nothing, to do with their lives and the decisions they make about them.

Except for major disasters, news channels focus on items occurring in their own geographic area or sub-culture. Furthermore, the competition for viewers encourages channels serving the same area to 'play it safe' by monitoring, and then mirroring, each other's coverage. Thus, most viewers, who do not trawl the channels on cable or satellite systems, receive a very narrow view of what is happening in the world and an even narrower view of the true causes and background. What they do see is presented from their local perspective. Advice is confined to experts close to the establishment. These do little more than summarise mainstream opinion, in terms of mainstream assumptions. When political disagreements are presented, marketing experts carefully prepare the parties. Political discussions become a battle to catch out each side; both saying as little as possible and giving no real answers. When a controversial figure breaks into the news, the dissenter is interviewed with incredulity. Little challenge to accepted opinion gets through.

Such imbalance of coverage inculcates dangerous assumptions in the public mind. A single death in our own country may be given massive coverage, but the slaughter of thousands elsewhere is considered hardly only worth a mention. A missing child in our national community may occupy days of headlines, whereas ongoing slavery and child soldiers (armed by weapons we make for profit) in faraway lands warrant only an occasional mention. Because we put ourselves and then our family first, we feel happier with parochial opinions that care little for strangers. We hardly know, let alone understand, them! Twenty-four-hour news can make the world seem like a global village, but when the big issues do erupt, the news channels' routine of narrow-base reporting can lead to partiality, or even prejudiced dismissal: 'Let's move on to something more important to us.' 'Foreigners', be they people overseas or from alien social groups in our own land, 'create their own problems for themselves (and us as well), don't they?'

Marketing for money
Nowhere, it seems, can we avoid being persuaded by agencies of the rich and privileged, who seek to buy their way into, and form, our minds.

- ❖ *Goods and services* : The practice of manipulating vulnerable minds for personal gain is at the core of exploitative capitalism. So, it is not surprising that the best paid strategists, artists and performers directly or indirectly work for the advertising industry. It was in the late 1950s that the industry incorporated psychological methods in a more intensely systematic way.[34] With the aid of television and radio, the ability to identify and pretend to answer people's deepest needs was irresistible. Using results produced by the latest statistical sampling, marketing techniques are fine-tuned to create and embark upon a surely successful public campaign.

- ❖ *Ideas and ideals*: As such methods proved successful in the commercial world, techniques were developed to market ideas, even ideals. Today's lobby groups devise ways to encourage the public to have the required opinion. Opinion polls and focus groups test public response, and then images are adjusted and tested again until the maximum opinion change is achieved. In such an enterprise, the morality and true needs of a project, possibility, person, political party or policy are of very little importance. Whether or how it can be made to be accepted is what we want to know and will pay good money for.

- *Sponsorship*: Marketing goes beyond TV to boards and electronic displays, dominating virtually every nook and cranny of public life. Sport, in many ways today's mass religion, is supported by commercial interests in exchange for showing display boards, electronic screens and exclusive logos at post-match interviews. Some agreements are bizarre. Producers of food and drink containing limited or no nutritional value market exclusively at great sporting events. Increasingly, commercial interest behind business sponsorship of schools and universities.

Entertainment

Neptune at its most sublime represents the spiritual inspiration found in great drama, music and art; soaring in wonder from our souls. Whatever our nature or interests, it is those recognisable total moments that touch us most deeply — empathising in joy, sadness or even terror — experiences that motivate the core of our decision-making processes. So, on television, fictional characters seem to share their lives with us: what they do, we would wish to do. Sounds ease or agitate our peace of mind, or urge us to act. Visions can stir us to great endeavours.

Pop idols can have cult status that inspires the very essence of our being. Some people watch television mindlessly all day. For others, entertainment can be the deadening opposite; just sound or vision in the background.

However we approach it, what is seen by millions on television can profoundly affect how the nation is, even what it believes and decides to do, or not to do. What are the crucial decisions to make, or questions to ask, or those we just cannot be bothered to ask? In so many ways popular media can be misused to confuse and seduce.

In 1950s Britain, commercial television was allowed amidst considerable controversy. Those against it argued that nothing is for free. Advertisers would pass their costs to consumers and standards would lower. The fears have been largely realised! Banal interruptions in transmissions to promote bubbly hair, anti-ageing cream, alcohol, laxatives, seductive aromas, junk foods and the like undermine key dramatic moments. To overcome the distraction, documentaries tend to summarise previous segments after each advertisement break. Personal moments in our creative experiences are bombarded by slick intrusions that reduce art and entertainment to cheap, indulgent, buy and sell games. The constant interruptions during programmes have established a numbing effect, making the viewer more a victim of what is being watched than an interactive participant. Before TV recording and the 32x fast forward button, viewers were near to zombie land. Product placement in programmes is more difficult to avoid. What is left to believe in, when it is considered normal to welcome strangers into the very heart of our homes to lie to us?

So much entertainment aims to do no more than titillate and fascinate; to focus any possible cathartic experience in very narrow controllable areas of social reaction. Is there no escape from the special interest groups that lie behind the commercialisation of entertainment?

The problem of politicians

Unfortunately, those who claim the right to represent us often exploit the more degenerate aspects and methods of the communications industry: manipulatively sugar-coating those easy answers and empty promises that lie at the very motivational core of contemporary politics. When things are difficult, politicians use television to blame opponents, while, at best, merely tinkering ineffectively around the edges of the problem. Hoping all the time that with the short news cycle it will fade from the public memory.

Far too many politicians are devoted to power to serve themselves, or to advance special interests. Even most of those intending to serve selflessly are still part of, or dependent upon, the legislative, expert, scientific or business interests that claim to know what is best for the people. Presented as 'real-world realist thinkers', in fact, their role is to be bulwarks resistant to any organisational alternative to the status quo.

Legitimately 'qualified' and financially strong, sitting comfortably in senior positions in industry and commerce, education, science, financial and regulatory control, the leaders of our society have no interest in radical change and hence no agenda to bring it about. Their response to immediate public concerns are short-term and piecemeal; mere stopgaps until actual change can be put off altogether. For sustaining the status quo is far more important than informing debate. The electorate's right to radical opinion thus emasculated, it is ripe to be exploited, and then carefully choreographed through the 'democratic' dance of occasional election campaigns.

To control the public mind as to what is an *acceptable* 'real world' agenda, carefully chosen focus groups are formed to discover what people can be persuaded to want, within a range acceptable to the politicians seeking election. Next is tested the best way to promote this 'want' to them, so they 'believe' it is deliverable! The findings are used to narrow down policy and its communication to consistent 'party line' campaign phrases. Fully in on the 'game', the media target anyone caught off script. The election campaign becomes reduced to tediously repeated buzz words. In the United Kingdom at the time of writing, it is 'hard-working families', 'the "safety" of the National Health Service', 'jobs', 'education,' 'immigration', 'cost of living', 'the deserving (or undeserving) poor'.

Feeling taken for granted, even betrayed, by such cynicism; recent electorates have been drawn along darker paths. An opportunist breed of politician rides on the back of globalisation trade issues, immigration and terrorism to exploit vulnerable voters. Giving full-throated simplistic voice to popular prejudices and fears, it constantly repeats unsubstantiated accusations against 'culprit' individuals and groups. Distortions and lies become slogan chants, so constantly repeated that they convince ever-larger crowds they must be true. Whipped-up crowd mania, reminiscent of 1930s fascism, becomes an intensely self-centred celebration of at last 'getting one back' on those who did, or will do this 'to me'.

Whichever way voters choose to be misled and collude in such a 'what is in it for me' agenda, they become as culpable for the broken political system, as those who seek to represent them. Promises made to gain election are made to be broken. Some politicians may be corrupt, but are they any more so than the people who base electing them on their own short-term interests? By voting for panderers, we elect representatives who take us to the lowest reaches of self-ignorance.

The intelligent voter uses astro-cycles
Astro-cycles show clearly the mindless futility of such a process. The way we innovate, our taste in fashion and belief, how we handle fear, whether we need to grow or consolidate, our personal needs and dispositions are not

determined by answering short-term desire, or even by this or that economic-political theories and social policy. As the cycles of the planets unfold, so will the general and personal needs of the time. So, good policy-makers must be flexible, but still trustworthy; unshakeably resolute in the way they stick to their principles, with long-term clarity in their decision-making. They must be courageous in the face of adversity, capable of changing agendas by convincing others there are better ways to achieve those principles.

As Neptune moves through Pisces and Uranus through Aries, the experience of suffering, and the impulsive need to prevent it, is leading to some pretty frightening short-term actions. Pluto in Capricorn making it worse: in some parts of the world, public execution and mass slaughter is the way to power. The United Kingdom, and many other western countries, is cursed with a blame culture. We accuse and marginalise strangers, perceiving them to be the creators of our problems: immigrants; the European Union; the rich blame the cost of welfare, citing residents of 'sink estates'; the poor blame bankers and foreign speculators in financial and property markets. Working people rail against exploitative job contracts and the increasing gap between Britain's better- and worse-off. Everyone blames politicians, their training and the dominance of public school education. Like *The Blind Men and the Elephant* in John Godfrey Saxe's poem, '... each was partly in the right, all were in the wrong!'

The root problem is selfishness and ignorance, wherever it appears. How do we resolve the errors of the past and deal with the dangers of the future? Is our economic recovery real, or are we just avoiding taking tough decisions? Is there a 'global race' to win, or just our minds and our physical world to destroy? No one person, group, policy or belief is to blame for our circumstances. As long as we vote in response to the nature and hype of the process, the blame lies, fair and square, entirely with ourselves.

Do we want fortress mentality to drive our relationships? Genuinely democratic elections are based on principles and accepting what is involved in achieving them. The dramatic reforms brought in by the post-World War Two Labour government emanated from principles accepted by the electorate and implemented at a time of great hardship. If the mentality of recent election strategies had been the mood of those times, the British National Health Service would never have been created. Effective principles are based not on excluding, but on including as many opinions and needs as possible. The more people a policy serves the more people will support the work to achieve it and, most important, the more meaningful will be our experience of implementing it.

Beneficial election campaigns and post-election negotiations emanate from effective use of the astro-events. Are the policies and strategies discussed take account of the profound economic consequences of Pluto in Capricorn until 2024? With Uranus in Aries until 2019, are proposed changes based on more than half-baked hope? With Neptune in Pisces until early 2026 is our 'gospel' one of accusation and guilt or kindly bringing people together? With (as I write) Saturn in Sagittarius until Christmas 2017, are we accepting that there is a great deal that just will not be possible? Are we confident that those we vote for will deal wisely with obstacles in their way? When Jupiter transited Leo in 2015, who was the natural leader and who just in it for the glory? When in Virgo the next year, did criticism and anxiety run riot, out of control? Who do you trust to stick to their word, when Mercury slows to retrograde, and all around them are back-tracking?

Developing the right political attitude
In the UK, US, indeed all over the world, too many cheap election campaigns proselytising selfishness have brought us to a jaded situation where most people vote 'holding their noses'. An increasing number will not vote at all. Is it

impossibly naive to ask for a political landscape where representatives do not manipulate circumstances to the narrow self-interest of their group and policy prejudices? Change comes when the electorate not only vote to reject this game, but also have the wisdom to see beyond any policies designed to exclude and isolate. We must vote for solutions, not personal gain. Intelligent compassion enriches the soul and expands the experience of joy. Nelson Mandela was a leader with sufficient courage to grasp the moment with such a vision. The film *Invictus* depicts the courage and status with which he turned around his own supporters, together with old enemies, in a sporting enterprise that brought great rewards.[35] Pushing our own line reinforces our problems and creates new ones. Solutions come when we draw people together to stand up for what is right, whatever seems to be against us.

In a genuine democracy, decisions would be based on the informed insight of both the people and their representatives. By selecting unbalanced facts to support preconceived opinions, today's system confuses rather than informs the electorate, even failing to give full information to those who implement policies and laws on our behalf.

What advice politicians seek is nearly always prejudicially selected from the established 'expert' assumptions in fashion at the time, allied with vested commercial interests. Where experts disagree, a cacophony of contradictory, prejudicially-selected bits and pieces turns most people away. They feel unable to do more than acquiesce in the status quo. In this way, the public will is 'instructed' by selected 'experts', rather than consulted. Because the public are considered to have no 'properly informed' standing, decisions we do not want will go through on the nod, often determined by scientific research, with little or no ethical regard built into its system.[36] Should this be how public need is determined? Surely scientists are servant technicians to serve public needs when required? It is the public, not the 'expert' view of 'reality' that should determine the kind of world we live in.

With Pluto in Capricorn, the commercial-political system is ripe for radical challenge to its status quo. All the outer planets are dangerously charged together for good or ill. Mass support for self-serving defensive barriers could hold back this force of change and keep the masses 'safely' fragmented in impotent terror.

Instead, people with individual courage need to combine and dedicate their collective wisdom to a common-good society. Every-step enables ever better ways into the future. Together we will build a movement that is continually judged by the good it does.

Chapter 7 - The Problem with the World

Every day, the number of people participating in or affected by the race to global destruction grows alarmingly. Developed western countries have been expanding industrialisation for more than two centuries. The production mania of increasing numbers of Indians, Chinese, other East Asians and South Americans has now been joined by Africans. In these emerging countries, entrepreneurs become remarkably wealthy by organising the masses to work long hours for little reward. Even those still trying to lead traditional lives are disturbed by outsiders destroying their environment for commercial gain.

From the sixteenth to twentieth centuries, the colonial model found and exploited vast resources by force of arms and religious self-righteousness. western colonialists moved people and materials around the world to the benefit of their investors, host country and its citizens. UK towns, such as London, Liverpool and Bristol especially, prospered. In the Empires, forests hundreds of years old were cleared to create farmlands that reared livestock and grew lucrative cash crops, while grand houses were built from the ancient wood. Other precious raw materials were taken, native servants employed, colonial administrations established. A complete overriding western way of life was imposed on top of long-standing traditional local ways.

Towards the middle of the twentieth century, this system had reached breaking point. In just a few decades, with little forethought for the consequences, colonies gained independence from their western 'masters'. This did not mean a return to the old tribal systems of rule, but the transference of the power-reins of colonial infrastructures (western models of government, law and military organisation) to westernised native officials. Some of these had previously worked under, others fought against, colonial power. The people of these new countries, voting for the first time, were left with the same exploitative capitalist system, containing all the flaws that have been exposed in previous chapters, now administered by inexperienced officials who were immediately exposed to commercial neo-colonialist corruption.

Ever keen to encourage and profit from the militarisation of political conflict, arms dealers moved in very quickly, supplying whichever sub-group could control the resources to pay for the weapons that would keep that group in power. Alongside the material temptations of the western system came also its educational and academic assumptions that increasingly side-lined traditional knowledge. A total return to the past was not considered a possibility. The ruling elite preferred the new western system as the modern way. They condemned the brutality and primitive nature of the old ways, even though before colonisation these traditions had stabilised their part of the world. Yet, while not in extrinsic power, the old tribal loyalties and cultures remained. The colonial powers had drawn many of the new nations' boundaries without regard to how they cut across these tribal territories. So, independence of colonial countries often led to tribal conflict. Resentment, even ethnic cleansing and retribution, was left unchecked and made more terrible with western weapons of war. These horrors, exacerbated in recent times by Islamic fundamentalist slaughter moving into vacuums left by ongoing conflict, are the consequence. To escape all this, millions of refuges flood to the borders of Europe. Payback time?

Ever-expanding world market place
Back in the world marketplace, with a foothold in just about every land, vast new potential markets have opened for multi-national companies. In the post-World War Two years, most western factories turned from weapons to the production of household convenience electrical goods; using

cheap raw materials, bought from the Third World, whose elite rulers often sold their resources for personal gain. The West did not have it to itself for long. Japan was the first non-western country to industrialise, followed by Hong Kong, South Korea, Taiwan and other South East Asian countries. At first the output was of rudimentary quality: 'Japanese cheap junk' became 'Hong Kong cheap junk' and so on. The highest standard of expertise was soon learned and prices became much lower than US and European workers' high living standards would allow.

We saw in Chapter 2 that China's late, but totally committed, entry into this mass production revolution has been both exciting and catastrophic for the western exploitative capitalist system. With vast wealth, both in natural and cheap human resources and excellent hard-working, productive skills, China and other Asian countries have undercut and flooded the world with every kind of consumer product. In exchange for raw materials, China has offered irresistible development deals to resource-rich countries. So, the production of consumer goods has grown exponentially.

The western world and its capitalist system face an ironic paradox. While some exploited and exploitable areas of the world remain (mainly in Africa and South America), many of the previously exploited countries are now exploiting the countries by whom previously *they* were exploited. This is having a seriously depressing effect on employment and prosperity in established western economies.

No room to breathe
In seeking a metaphor for the condition of the present world economy, we can remind ourselves of, and develop the image of, the trawler fishing net drawing in and tightening around its catch, which was evoked in the introduction. At first the net gently surrounds the shoal of fish. Then, as it

eases them toward each other, the larger fish feed on the smaller ones and the even-larger ones feed on both. As the net opens and throws its contents on the deck, all the horror is revealed of fish in the mouth of fish in the mouth of an even larger fish, all caught in the act of eating one another, as they desperately gasp for breath and die in an unsustainable environment.

It is becoming just like this on our planet: resources are not unlimited. As more and more parts of the world join today's exploitative world economy (not only competing in industrial production, but also in unproductive speculative financial trading and avoidance strategies), what is available to sustain us diminishes. Entities (countries and corporations) eat not only each other but the planet itself. First the coal, then the oil, gas (shaking the very fabric of the ground to squeeze [frack] out the last drops), special metals and other raw materials. We use up natural products, wood, stripping the land, causing erosion and distorting the cycle of nature, choking up the air with poisonous gases, cluttering up space with bits of satellites. Yet still, frantic leaders urge citizens that the only solution to their problems is to group together in this ever-more-crowded world. We must be the best against all the others in a race to be ever busier, to consume, to 'succeed', to 'win' the race to global destruction!

Defending 'our way of life'
The immediacy of international communications that enhance understanding and intensify this global race brings us closer to its dangers. As resources and room for manoeuvre in this business world diminish, we feel threatened and naturally seek protection. It can take many forms. Rules to keep out what might threaten are always open to interpretation and dependent upon the honour of the parties. Sanctions and enforcement are more likely to endanger than defend. The relationship between people and

police forces and armies will depend more upon might than truth. Business dealings easily degenerate into the best means to defend what we have. Where there are conflicts of interest, those in power prevent open debate. The rich tend to live in special areas, often behind guarded secure walls and fences. Where there is racial conflict, the dominant army may try to put a protective wall around a whole country.

Whoever decides and administers borders and the lands they contain can endanger rather than protect. Where African and Middle East countries, created by western colonial edicts, cut across tribal and religious loyalties, often minorities rule by force of arms.

The horror of unresolved, maybe irresolvable, conflict disrupts and then destroys the lives of ordinary people. The numbers of the needy constantly increase and wander in search of places that offer safety and opportunity. Dangers caused by difference and distribution knock on our door. We care, but do we care sufficiently to act enough to solve the problem and bring the peoples of the world together? For most, it is too complex to understand what we did (and continue to do) to cause the sufferings of these foreign people, and what we 'owe' them in return.

The amoral exploitative capitalist system desensitises societies. When room for manoeuvre runs out, it can sour natural kindness to not caring. People then can be persuaded to act on the assumption that everyone is in it for themselves. Yet the need to care and be cared for always lies deep in the consciousness, not only of humans but of all nature. Tolerance is how the bodies in the heavens move around each other. We may have to kill to live, but we do not have to hate, disrespect and persecute our victim while doing so, or to kill for little or no reason. Yet this is what our exploitative capitalist system seems to legitimise all the time. To have and have more, to indulge beyond satisfaction, to titillate and expose, to push the boundaries of outrageous display and licentiousness. The privileged countries seem to be parading such freedoms in full sight of a world where most are dispossessed and suffering and evermore likely to be so. No wonder that hundreds of thousands struggle through deserts and dangerous oceans for their share, only to be met at first with, at best, embarrassed sympathy, and ultimately seen as a danger to defend ourselves against.

Losing our young people
The perceived hypocrisy and injustice of any society drives its young generation to dramatic rebellion in many ways. In the 1930s, millions joined Hitler Youth, while others fought fascism in Spain and then joined armies in World War Two. In the 1960s and early 1970s, the brutality of their fathers turned US and European youth against the Vietnam War. In Mao's communist China, his *Little Red Book* led a generation to inform on their parents and deny their spiritual heritage. In the late 70s, punk rockers proselytised destructiveness, while in the 1980s Yuppies worshiped monetarism. In the 1990s, the young sired an electronic revolution, which was to take over world communications in the new century. Then came the Islamic counter-revolution, as an absolute rejection of global displays of wealth and sexual liberation. With brutal uncompromising puritanism, it insisted upon a return to a highly literal interpretation of Sharia Law.

It may be at the extreme opposite to the 1960s peace and free-love youth rebellion, but it is important to realise that the attraction of Isil's uncompromising message also touches a similar naive idealistic chord in the heart of some young Muslims. Maybe its message can seem relevant to a vulnerable minority of the generation brought up in the uncertain Islamic sub-cultural sidelines of amoral, materialistic western society, with its vision of purposeless competitive success. Much is said about countering the problem of Isil's grooming of innocent young minds. Not enough is said about how the amorality of our culture, and especially our materialist education, can prepare the ground for such grooming. When so much information is mechanical and amorally functional, and so little school time spent on socially-inclusive value judgements, what is more attractive to a naive, innocent mind: a university degree leading to debt and possibly no more than a zero-hours contract job, or fighting to destroy what seems to be an unjust and aimlessly licentious culture—especially when you believe in the certainty of heaven at the end of the quest?

For the exploitative capitalist system is not the benign, tolerant of all faiths and cultures, democratic, one-size-fits-all way of organising our affairs for the benefit of all. It is a belief system of what is and is not real. It believes in the prime importance of the material world, and structures discovery, educational systems, rewards and recognition accordingly. It sees life as a struggle to survive, which should be undertaken according to agreed rules. Yet these rules may be bent and even broken in the cut and thrust of social interaction; all a part of the 'game'. Success is measured in terms of outcomes, especially material possession, victory and other endgame icons of recognition that are esteemed fashionable from time to time.

Those who reject this belief system consider and treat it as no more than a resource to attack and feed off; dangerously violent terrorism, imprisonment, torture and assassination ensue.

The amorality of the exploitative capitalist system means that it is ever ready to profit from the dysfunctional and corrupt mentalities that surround such situations. Weapons exchanged for valuables, be they legal or illegal, can give power to the most brutal and unreasonable groups of people, who believe that their fight is just as justified as the way world powers defend their special interests. Political sub-groups in countries may also be supplied by nations, cynically seeking surrogates to serve their own personal agendas. Lines are drawn, across which it is certainly dangerous, often impossible, to pass. Understanding fades, even shatters. Positions become ever more rigid and retractable. Twenty-four-hour world communication systems show us more and more of what there is to hate about each other.

The consequences of our amoral belief system

The western technical revolution, powered by the didactic functionality of its education system, has been the driving force of the global race over recent centuries. Now this system has been adopted enthusiastically by today's emerging economies, the pace of the race quickens. In South East Asia, children attend school conscientiously and then study for many hours after into the evening.[37] In this way, in-built amorality is initiated into millions, if not billions more people. Traditional cultures may remain more resilient than in the West, but these 'old ways' are regarded as separate, existing alongside the new way. Especially in China, where family associations are important, most workers work vast distances away, to earn enough to send funds home. As for most people, the global race undermines our time with those closest to us. Life becomes unnatural, a treadmill, a necessity to hate; exploitation of the 'have nots' by the 'haves'.

In any race, there are only a few winners. Most try nearly as hard, but end up losing. In a race that is often skewed in favour of those who have already succeeded, either materially or intellectually, vast numbers will be barely surviving in sink groups; this could be the majority in the poorer countries. Living off food banks and out of date produce, the poor in western societies are still more fortunate compared to people displaced by war, created by injustice and fanatical reactions to it. We have seen how the extreme imbalances of opportunity between rich and poor people and areas of the world are leading to a growing mass refugee crisis. People are desperate to use any means to break through the barriers barring entry to rich countries.

The needs of such millions of people are counter-intuitive to the exploitative capitalist system, which considers that to help those who cannot help themselves will sustain 'their failed life patterns'. They will become an inefficient, dysfunctional burden on the system, both within and between countries. People as individuals and mass groups must be left to suffer. Such attitudes leave the world economy with a calculation for which it is not equipped: the financial consequences of policing and armies to contain mass emigration, revolution, terrorism and war. For so many clear and simple reasons, every element of our global economic system is not fit for purpose.

Everyone has the solution to all their conflicts.
So here is our world right now. Many people certain of the rightness of their contradictory wrong answers; fighting battles, over which their opponents will never allow them the final victory; living unhappy lives within the culture they struggle against all odds to preserve; seeking victories that can never be more than empty.

For, if the exploitative capitalist system could survive and grow, it would eat the world and its people alive; continually consuming natural resources, ravaging the fabric of the planet and throwing pollution into the atmosphere. The captains of corporate world commerce and their legal, educational and political supporters would drive suffering populations into believing that they must work and consume ever more. For some never-properly-explained reason, this is the only way to enjoy a promised happiness that is always just over the horizon. In fact, it leads to worn out people collapsing exhausted in a barren, infertile world.

If instead, or even as well, enmity builds to bloody battles, modern technology ensures they will be fought amidst unbelievable death and destruction. Look at how it is, right now, in places where either side dominates.

In our heart of hearts, no one wants it this way. Few are fighting or supporting fighters because war is what we want. Nearly all during war cry nightly for it to end.

Be reassured! Everyone involved has the solution to all their conflicts at their very finger tips. It involves realising that in their hearts only the most deluded and damned in any culture seek death, destruction, the harming of and stealing from others as a way of life. *We* feel we must be this way, because *they* are *that* way. But *they* are not *that* way; *they* feel they must be *that* way, because *we* are *that* way.

The solution is to refuse to see things like this, to seek and find that kind heart, not just in our friends, but in our enemies as well; to be kind towards all near and far, and to the planet; to refuse to join the race to global destruction.

The rest of this book will explain more precisely how a better world can come to be.

Part Two

Reversing
 the Race to Global Destruction

Chapter 8 - Finding Answers to All Our Problems

When faced with a problem the wise do not rush to solve it, but apply themselves assiduously to a deep study of its nature and interconnected contributory factors. Having done this in *Part One*, we are armed with such clarity that all knee-jerk reactions and piecemeal solutions should fade before they start. Anchored uncompromisingly at the heart of the problem, we are ready for real, strong solutions to begin to take shape.

The momentum of history advances like a large vessel through water, insistent to continue on its way, slow and reluctant to accept change and turn, until it confronts an immovable object. Then, often too late to transform into something even better, fixed mindsets seek to sustain the past, by railing and barging against each other. Each side in the flow takes matters to destructive excess, leaving a world bruised from all sides. Those who remain pick up the pieces as best they can.

The rise and fall of great empires
To date, it has been the pattern of history for great empires to emerge, grow and dominate by means of wondrous innovations and efficient organisational power; only to expand to an over-confident climax. At this point, when the established imperial ways appear to be inviolate, an unexpected, overlooked, even deliberately disregarded or dismissed force starts the process of bringing the assumed-impregnable edifice crashing down. In ancient Babylon, Nebuchadnezzar was confronted by the writing on the wall. The Persian Empire fell to the jumped-up youth of Alexander the Great, who himself was to die shortly before his 34th birthday. The divine heritage of Egyptian pharaohs was defeated by Rome, and then its rule of the then known world was destroyed by outsider invaders, bursting in on its self-indulgent licentiousness and intolerant religious

schisms. In the thirteenth century, the cultural wonder that was ancient Baghdad fell to Mongols. In the fifteenth and sixteenth centuries, resurgent Christianity pushed back Islam's rule in Spain. The Ottoman Empire's defeat in World War One halted its expansion into Mongols, yet also saw the end of Christian imperial families in Austria-Hungary, Prussia and Russia; even Britain during the decades that followed. How are the mighty fallen!

The sinking of RMS *Titanic* is an incisive illustration of how the dominant cultures of the twentieth century had warnings, but failed and fell because they ignored them; Instead, they preferred to glory and see divine permanence in their mission to rule the world.

A wondrous product of the massive advances in the technology of the time, the vessel seemed set fair to herald in a new era of global travel. It was fitted out with the most luxurious comforts that hubris could imagine. Its engines could cross the Atlantic faster than ever before. Above all it was considered unsinkable, until that horrible iceberg moment of truth for all on board. Ironically, it was the very luxury that distracted the radio operator from receiving iceberg warnings from other ships, instead telegraphing the passengers' paid-for 'meeting-on-arrival' arrangements, as the liner sped ever-faster to its too-late-heeded collision

This disaster was the unheeded herald of far worse times to come. Within less than three years, the pumped-up arrogant competition between European industrial powers to dominate and colonise the world led them to create unyielding solid walls of mass death on the western Front of World War One. More than 100 years on, in the twenty-first century, we continue to struggle to come to terms with the consequences of this insane international hubris.

Will consumer capitalism go the same way?
Certainly, the first seven chapters have questioned whether our assumed modern world view is any more permanent.

Chapter 2 suggests the period until the mid-2020s will be a radical test. Should disaster rip us apart, the consequences would be far more devastating and the room for recovery far more difficult to find than ever before. Paradoxically, it is the brilliance of our achievements, mastering so many corners of the world and using up so much of its resources, that bring this very danger. The higher the knowledge and more powerful the instrument, the far greater is responsibility and far direr the consequences if it is not honoured.

Yet, there is good news. The disastrous end to eminent imperial cultures in the past only happened because the people in those times were too arrogant to face the dangers and act to adapt in time. The Persians did not need to invade Ancient Greece and so encourage retaliation. If the Council of Nicaea had come to less didactic conclusions, the Roman Empire may not have divided. If political involvement and the sale of indulgences had not dominated the fifteenth century Roman Church, Christian schism and conflict may not have been the story of the millennia that followed. The imperial nations of twentieth century Europe could have put aside their greed and vindictiveness towards each other. Instead they could have celebrated and cooperated in their imperial good fortune, constantly improving the lot of the nations they administered.

Such disasters do not have to happen. There are always advance warnings, ways of turning around to avoid the wrong way for an enterprise, society or even a whole world. The Titanic received, but ignored warnings of icebergs ahead, because the sending of passenger greetings took precedent. Now today, the economic trauma of 2008 (following on from our ignoring the warning of 2000 and the 1989-92 recessions) was a Pluto-in-Capricorn last-ditch demand for proper global efficiency, before the end of the decade and into the early 2020s.

It is rarely too late to put change in motion. Although it seems unlikely to be effective at first, little movements in the right direction can start the ship, enterprise, the world economy, and society moving positively forward. These will gather in momentum and confidence as persistence makes us take hold of the process and moves the 'ship' around; 'the journey of a thousand miles starts with a single step.'[38]

The first step of a new way

Uncompromising honesty in its deepest, most courageous sense is that first vital step we need to take, so we can face and answer the demands of our times. To act this way is the key to the gate that opens the way to all solutions.

By identifying what is wrong, certainly we were not seeking to make a case to go back to the past, but it is vital to learn from it. Especially, we should remind ourselves of the eternal values people then ignored, and so allowed in the disaster that befell them. Today, we are much more advanced. What we need now is to balance our advances, so we can progress to the highest standards necessary to accommodate them. The earlier chapters gave hints of possible solutions. Now we must combine and develop them into viable strategies. We do not seek to go back, but to advance to a more balanced, efficient and sustainable future.

> This above all; to thine own self be true
> And it must follow, as does the night the day
> Thou cans't not then be false to any man[39]

In the Christian and Jewish faiths, God knows our innermost thoughts. In Islam, ever-obedient angels record every deed and action. Eastern religions are centred on a rigorous understanding of cause and effect, known as karma. Each comes down to a central, unavoidable reality – in the end, you can't get away with anything!

Everything we think, say and do creates the cause for an inevitable outcome. So why are we so stupid as to think we can institutionalise, even legalise, ways of destroying, lying, robbing, cheating, exploiting, harming, dominating, oppressing, avoiding, ignoring, confusing and otherwise spoiling the happiness of each other, without suffering future consequences? How can serious, responsible reductionist scientists rip apart the planet with little thought for future consequences? How can practical economists, with their intricate theories of avoidance, and the proud realistic top business barons who employ them, consider that the institutionalisation of greed and deceit will have no negative consequences? How can some of the best educated brains in our world be mainly focused on short-term methods to exploit and harm our planet? How can the most sensitive and talented artists be happy to grow rich by prostituting their art in the service of mass deception and exploitation, or give up and degenerate into neat displays of self-indulgent psychosis? How can the politicians who wish to represent us be more interested in being elected than telling the truth and solving our problems? How can such a world, run by such people with an assumed air of being efficient, qualified, righteous in their expert knowledge and right to rule, be considered, in any way, efficient and fit for purpose?

Of course, they are not fit for purpose and (make no mistake) nor are we who allow them to rule. Realising this, and saying so, is the first step to finding a solution. The earlier chapters have shown that flawed individuals administer the world, with flawed motivation, theories and systems that are the inefficient cause of their failure. Pluto's transit through Capricorn represents the last years of a system that in the past succeeded for some despite its cruelty towards the many, but now is coming to its sell-by date for all of us.

Not fit for purpose
It would have been wonderful if the speculative capitalist system could have expired during the depression of the 1930s and been replaced by a principled free-enterprise

system. Instead, relaxing the strict relationship between the US currency and gold enabled the adoption of seductive ways to extend the apparent money supply. It opened a refuge in times of difficulty. Today it dangerously moves us far beyond anything Keynes would have visualised.

To allow people to have and trade symbolic money with no firm basic collateral is an open door to creative accounting and price manipulation. Certainly, the New Deal in the US necessarily financed projects to get the economy moving again. The extension of credit after World War Two helped to restore the world economy, particularly for the defeated countries, but how would have things gone if the war had not intervened? Expansion of the money supply is an emergency strategy, not the fundamental way to administer an economy. While it is good to be able to borrow through difficult times, debts must be repaid. Basing the world economy on the constant expansion of debt can but accelerate the race to global destruction.

Attempts to keep up with the quickening pace of economic demand have dominated the way we think, learn, work, listen, follow others and are entertained. Like jugglers, we are desperately driven to keep up and sustain the unrealistic ungrounded nature of our lives. With no tangible standard by which to measure what we think and do, we just keep on doing. We become slaves to whatever force of action or opinion seems to dominate the time.

The *Golden Standard*

Of course, the physical ownership of gold was not and cannot be the righteous foundation of an auspicious and stable economy. It certainly was not during those 1879-1933 Gold-Standard years for Britain, or for the US when it finally left the standard in the 1970s. Its value was the way it represented a limitation on how far we could go, how much we could extend credit and hence the true value of the economy. That the 1920s boom led to the 1929 Wall Street

Crash was not a reason to abandon the Gold Standard, but to learn and adapt. A wise world would have gone further and seen the need for the kind of Gold Standard this book now argues for today.

Perhaps we should call it the *Golden Standard*, because it is about much more than material things; rather, *principles by which we relate to and do business with each other*. Free dealing between people in enterprise and all other human interactions must be the very best way, but all dealings must be based on generally accepted and honoured principles. Throwing delicious sweets in the air before excited children is little different to giving a delicious sandwich to a greedy flock of gulls. With no way of dealing with right and wrong, the diving pack will fight and struggle to have the most. Maybe talking to the gulls in advance would make little difference, but a word to the children, about making sure everyone has enough, could.

In suggesting we establish, prize and keep untarnished even more than gold the principles by which we live our lives, we echo the essence of Confucius' view that men's relationship with men is the measure of all things. With the edict 'what you do not wish for yourself do not do to others', he both echoed and anticipated the timeless Golden Rule of so many spiritual masters.

The key to the Confucian approach is its placing emphasis not on rules, which were uncertain and prone to circumvention, but on the central principle that motivated an action. The intention of an act is far more important than any rule broken in the committing of it. A perfectly ordered harmonious society could come from the acts of human beings, provided they followed principles and did not hide behind or seek advantage from rules. Every situation had to be considered in its context and judged by discerning the motivating principle behind each action.

Another crucial distinction was his insistence that the best principles, such as integrity, loyalty and respect, came from moral values to be found in good family relationships. Confucius placed much reliance on a time when the Duke of Zhou's kingdom was ruled with perfect principle. Because all his people were treated as he would treat his own family, a most happy, harmonious social order was created in his kingdom.

In all times, good men should not devote themselves to personal gain. If rulers become corrupt in this way, nature will show their failure by bringing natural disaster. If this happens the people have the right to rebel.

Not the *Golden Standard*

What we saw in earlier chapters shows that today's society turns the Confucian ideal upside down. It restricts the time modern families can spend together and focuses education on self-interest, rather than caring for the world as a family. Indeed, the way we administer and adjudicate our contemporary life is much more akin to the ideas of Machiavelli, who Wikipedia cites as the founder of modern political science and ethics. Quotations from his groundbreaking *The Prince* have a frighteningly pertinent ring in the modern world.

- It is better to be feared than loved, if you cannot be both...If an injury has to be done to a man it should be so severe that his vengeance need not be feared...A battle that you win cancels any other bad action of yours.
- It is undoubtedly necessary for the ambassador occasionally to mask his game; but it should be done so as not to awaken suspicion and he ought also to be prepared with an answer in case of discovery.
- A prince ought to have no other aim or thought, nor select anything else for his study, than war and its rules and discipline; for this is the sole art that belongs to him who rules, and it is of such force that it not only upholds those who are born princes, but it often enables men to rise from a private station to that rank.

More charmingly ironic, but just as pertinently ruthless are the Ferengi *286 Rules of Acquisition*,[40] well known to followers of *Star Trek*. Below are just a few.

13. Anything worth doing is worth doing for money
14. Anything stolen is pure profit
20. When the customer is sweating, turn up the heat
21. Never place friendship before profit
27. The most beautiful thing about a tree is what you do with it after you cut it down
28. Morality is always defined by those in power

Dealing with each other, as we now do, according to such principles, we ensure that disharmony increasingly dominates both within and without sub-cultures, societies and countries throughout the world.

Implementing the *Golden Standard*

The Confucian antidote to all this was that society should listen to the most virtuous and follow their lead, whatever their position in society. Such people would have developed a quality that he called 'Ren', human-heartedness. The more this key quality is developed, the more its elite status will emerge and direct our way.

In the twentieth century, Chögyam Trungpa motivated courage for self-improvement by explaining the nature of an ideal community— Shambhala.

> It is not just an arbitrary idea that the world is good, but it is good, because *we can experience it as goodness*...Shambhala vision is trying to provoke you to understand how you live, your relationship with ordinary life...the essence of warriorship, or the essence of human bravery is refusing to give up on anyone or anything.[41]

Chögyam Trungpa's understanding comes from the Tibetan tradition, developed from Gautama Buddha, a contemporary of Confucius. This Indian spiritual leader crystallised human-heartedness into five key compassionate precepts to prevent harm. We should avoid all acts in which we kill, steal, lie, self-confuse with intoxicants or abuse others sexually, because they have dire consequences that cause great suffering; not only to those others, but ourselves as well. To do such things is the worst, but to express the wish or encourage others to do them is nearly as bad. Even to wish like this in our minds has negative karmic consequences.

It is both curious and highly significant that many western people misunderstand the notion of karma, suggesting that to say something is subject to karma is a 'cop out'; an attempt to avoid responsibility. These are usually those who see nature as intrinsically cruel and arbitrary. So they prepare our children for life by educating them to lie, steal and kill if necessary as they battle to survive. At the same time, they extol the pleasures of violent adventure, sexual indulgence and 'legally'-defined intoxicants — usually alcohol.

The very opposite is the case. The Eastern view of karma holds that everything that happens is the result of previous actions, words or thoughts. We cannot blame anyone but ourselves for anything. When we accept karmic consequences, and apply such standards to our own lives, we may begin to understand where and why we went wrong before. When we apply them to every social action, public utterance, policy statement, brutality and justification in the public arena, we can see how we and our representatives consistently dig us ever deeper into a grave of terrifying, seemingly inescapable despair. Listen to their words! What are they doing and encouraging us to do? Watch the news, read newspapers, ponder the cumulative consequences of each deliberate distortion, encouragement to denigrate and harm, deliberately wrong-footing and misrepresenting. See brutality and ignorant intransigence rise as the dominant extol and celebrate their power. The weak are left powerless, to cringe and suffer, or to be exploited by fanatics with simplistic solutions that will only make matters worse.

To recognise and avoid rushing counter productively down paths that harm others and so ourselves, it is helpful to identify the states of mind that cause such behaviour. Buddhists call them the Eight Worldly Dharmas. Seeing happiness as coming from the five senses and attaching our minds to the satisfaction of these senses, we grasp with all our might after gain, happiness, fame and praise. At the same time, we do all we can to avoid loss, unhappiness, notoriety and criticism.

At first sight this seems reasonable. Surely to abandon the Eight World Dharmas would lead to a miserable, unsuccessful life, full of disappointment! Paradoxically, it is quite the opposite. For it is not what we have or how we are perceived that creates happiness and unhappiness, but the way our minds take on board what happens. Following on from this, it is this dissatisfaction in our minds that triggers us into taking the very negative actions that come back to harm us, when the karma of those actions ripens. Even before then, it is the intuitive subconscious realisation, the anticipation of this danger of 'cosmic payback' that continually haunts our minds, triggering and amassing more negative actions that themselves will have karmic consequences.

In this way, the tragedy of individuals and nations proceeds and intensifies. Our need for sensual satisfaction takes refuge in the growth of possessions, of profit and the rules to protect what is ours. Fear of loss builds barriers to be attacked or defended in wars, where all are losers living in a wasteland.

We will feel better as soon as we stop such wrong actions, feel confident enough to let down defensive barriers and allow the world to become a friendlier place. Then we will stop labelling people and situations as friends, enemies and strangers. By looking deeply and objectively, we will see each has been both help and hindrance to our happiness many times over. So, all begin to feel better as the consequences created by negative karma lessen. Starting with tiny steps at first, relaxing light will grow in our minds and, as it does, our personal world and maybe even *the* world will start to get better.

Adopting the *Golden Standard*
About 2,500 years ago, Confucius offered Ren human heartedness and Gautama Buddha offered non-harming compassion, as the way to heal his contemporary wayward society. It was then and remains today the *Golden Standard* by which to base, judge and decide all our actions. So, as then, in the twenty-first century we must embark on a process of changing our mindset if we are to survive and be happy.

May the extent of our compassion be the measure of success in all we do!

Chapter 9 - Applying Answers to All Our Problems

We suffer from an overload of rules and regulations. The more we have the less effective these are and the more they separate us from each other. Of course, there are natural laws that define the individuality and nature of people, places and processes. Each of us is unique, with our own tastes, likes and dislikes. There is a vast difference between the hectic heaving nature of a large city and a peaceful countryside field. Hydrogen and oxygen do combine to make water and, with the right conditions, always will be separated by hydrolysis. One of the joys in life is to learn and work with the vast varieties of existence.

However, problems arise when, with brute force, we seek to block out people or deny natural rules, when we put up artificial barriers, seeking to force others and the world around us to serve our interests. Unnatural barriers separate and confuse the flow of relationships. They cause distortions in the material world, such as pollution and shortage of resources. From barriers comes resentment between people; a cruel abuse to that natural inborn kindness that can make us feel safe just about anywhere we are.

Principles are rules that unify
In *Part One*, we learned that *tolerance* is the underlying principle holding everything together at all levels of the Universe. Out there in space, in nature and our societies on Earth, within our innermost selves, tolerance is the way. Seeking to confront and eradicate opponent forces is counter productive. The stronger can destroy their attackers, but even the most successful belligerent is never more than one opponent away from defeat. It is far better to follow the planets, stars and galaxies. Work around, accommodate contrary forces, make them complementary. By avoiding extreme power and evil that cannot be changed, we leave difficult circumstances to consume themselves in their own

loneliness. If you just cannot help, contain the fire until it burns out and dies.

Because this is so, if they are to be effective, rules in our world must be based on a generally-accepted ethical foundation. There must be deep principles that emphasise compliance with the very essential spirit of the law, not a manipulated case-law-created shell of closely argued 'letter of the law' ifs and buts. Furthermore, to give it fundamental lasting integrity, this essential foundation must apply, and be seen to apply, to everyone equally throughout society.

It must be administered with honesty, as well as compassionate understanding, but we do not pander to people's self-deceiving special pleading. Although rules should be applied flexibly subject to principle, this is no soft options: no avoiding the consequences by pretending to have good intentions. The intrinsic truth of karma underlies the outcome of all decisions and actions: there is no escape. When verdicts and especially sentencing are dependent upon principles, no issue can be left unresolved. All parties must be fully satisfied with the outcome, or work on it until they are. Failure to do this will leave negative karmic consequences that will grow and ripen for the parties and society. Achieving reconciliation will lead to ever-growing immeasurable happiness for all involved, both in the immediate situation and faraway places and times.

So, we need to identify and place principles at the heart of every element of our dealings. They will override rules and laws that will become no more than practical guidelines to what is generally expected. Did we act in that way? Why? How close or far away from the *Golden Standard* the action is should decide the punishment or redress, not whether an offender has or has not stuck to 'the letter of law'.

Establishing a principle-based system of legal precedent

At first sight, the suggestion that we should make such a radical change to the emphasis of statute and common law precedent, established over hundreds of years, may seem profoundly naive. To lawyers and law-makers such a new focus may seem an unrealistic, crassly conceived path that would open the doors to social anarchy.

Yet, how different in scale to the legal complexities of the current system would be a system where the details and reference to precedent were argued based on the principles behind behaviour? Both depend upon interpretation. The current system tests the ability and persistence of the parties to argue the obscurities of legal precedent. The new suggestion is that we assess the offence by considering why a person acted as he or she did. Not only what harm or benefit it caused, but what was intended. Was the action taken responsibly with a good heart? A Sufi story tells of a wise man suddenly crossing the road to push down the high wall of the garden to an old lady's house, justifying his actions by showing that the wall would have fallen on and killed her the next day.

Focusing on principle and motivation opens the door to considering offences based on intention. Although there was no wrongdoing within a narrow definition of the law, did the perpetrator, unkindly or without regard to the consequences, intend to harm or do harm to an individual or society? If so, there should be power to enforce redress.

Using *Golden Standard* principles to improve sentencing

Relying on *Golden Standard* principles and intention rather than rules and laws as the final arbiter should be introduced step by step, drawing on and enhancing procedures in the existing system. Already at present, judges consider mitigating circumstances when sentencing. Rather than this being the judge's arbitrary judgement call, a system of case law could be built, based on the success and failure of previous decisions. This would grow to be the absolute decisive core of the final sentence. The circumstances of the offence and outcomes of what happened would be the key things to bear in mind. Conciliation and reconciliation would be the basis to deliver mutually satisfactory resolutions. Was there genuine regret, a wish to give redress? Would this redress be acceptable to the injured party? The process would require all involved to honour the principles of the *Golden Standard*, upon which decisions are based. Such an approach would not lead to soft options. Under a principled system, many who escaped justice will now face it. If there is no genuine regret, or wish to compensate, sentences may be more severe. As far as possible all prisoners should work and cover the expense of their incarceration, so the cost to society is recompensed. On the other hand, if process of genuine regret and compensation is agreed by the parties and delivered to the satisfaction of all concerned, then this may well be sufficient punishment. The central requirement would be monitoring to ensure that all parties are fully satisfied with the outcome and continue to feel this way. Payments by offenders and savings in the prison budget would finance the monitoring.

Many offenders in the criminal system and losing civil litigants could return to their lives. They could then benefit the victim and society by putting right the consequences of unprincipled wrong that they did. In such a system, intransigent unrepentant offenders will be dealt with as, if not more severely, than before. Crucially, there would be far fewer prisoners and few, if any, people unfairly or unnecessarily incarcerated.

Building up a new kind of case law and precedent
In the new way, the arguments will be as intricate as the old way, but the ongoing intention and the outcomes are diametrically different. In the present system justice is often left undone. It is more like a younger brother struggling to be heard. Winning is everything in that adversarial world: truth a legal definition, not an intrinsic principle. Few

allowances are made. Outcomes frequently leave one or even both sides feeling cheated.

Shifting the focus from the complex nuances of legal precedent and arguable procedures to the heart principle truth of the circumstances is much more likely to satisfy all parties. Transforming the current system to precedents, resting upon the motivation behind and the consequences of an action, would be far more effective, as well as acceptable.

Such a massive change would be brought in gradually. Rather as preventing smoking in some public places edged its way in, until the mood of most people towards it had changed far enough to allow its banning in all public places. When the intention behind actions is the key factor in deciding redress, everyone would be much more mindful of their own actions and far less cockily hiding behind 'It's not against the law' in all the mean things they do.

An interesting example of how to start is the way that the principle of the Overriding Objective is enshrined in Part 1 of the English and Welsh Civil Procedure Rules, to underlie consideration the rules that follow. It can be a core refuge when interpretation is uncertain. Similarly, we could build a body of precedent from Golden Standard principles.

Punishment, based on redress acceptable to both perpetrator and victim rather than fixed tariffs, would enable just and effective outcomes. Massive improvement in rehabilitation would ensue. In civil disputes, reconciliation would be easier, and with less time wasted.

All parties would feel the system is listening and seeking to resolve issues, not play a game with their futures. Society will become a fairer, happier place, with the principled rewarded and unprincipled put in their place.

A right relationship with the world and each other

A key resource in the establishment of the *Golden Standard* is the way we know and come to know what we discover, research, teach and then disseminate throughout society.

In recent decades, scientific innovation has been increasingly the major driving force of the world economy. So, the potential for economic reward very often focuses the allocation of research funding. In this way, short-to-medium-term economic considerations determine much of what we know and even the way we think about and see the world.

This is especially so in the pharmaceutical industry, where the likelihood of profitable outcomes can determine whether research takes place at all; be it for low-priced alternative health products or even diseases where allopathic remedies are essential. Before the 2013 outbreak, protection against Ebola was not considered a cost-justified area for research. For decades, the tobacco industry financed research that downplayed the potential danger of their product. Academic fashion can also determine research funding, so even pure scientific research may not operate on an even playing field. Theories in vogue, held by established figures, are more likely to be supported. In time, we may come to see the Large Hadron Collider as such an example. Then, to what extent is government-funded research determined by the political wishes of itself and its supporters?

For this range of reasons vast sums are spent on scientific research that provides us with a fascinating, fast-growing range of new understandings and methods to change our lives for the better or worse; a supermarket of wonderful possibilities. It is our amazing toolbox for modern living, but, as we saw in Chapter 4, it does not have the depth or ethical foundation to be the philosophy to live our lives by. Yet that is what it is becoming and what its most fanatical adherents insist it should be; saying to think otherwise is to live in the Dark Ages.

All research is not the same. What is popularly seen as scientific research today is just one way of researching. It is known as quantitative, because it aims to establish, contest and adapt facts to specific usable linear processes by means of carefully-calculated statistical observation. While much of such science is focused on the highest ethical intentions maybe to heal illness or avert ecological disaster, the wish for a specific outcome, whether beneficial or not, cannot be a part of a truly objective research study. By its very nature quantitative research is intrinsically amoral.

To assist ethical judgements research needs to be qualitative. It needs to explain and educate informed debate by observing and looking for associations, manifestations and analogies. When undertaken with a Confucian approach, it is a vital informant of the extent to which the *Golden Standard* is being applied.

Some of the most fruitful contemporary research is conducted when quantitative and qualitative approaches combine to study global warming and other environmental issues. When hard facts meet heartfelt values regarding the quality of life, even survival, contemporary science is at its very best.

Yet, self-interest-based quantitative scientism is the fundamentalist secular belief system that dominates education today. It not only affects the focus and funding of higher education, but vitally the pupils' experience of our school curriculum. We saw in Chapter 4 that subjects providing basic tools to compete in the quantitative business world (language, mathematics and science skills) are prioritised as core and their standards tested regularly. Competitive sport is preferred. Subjects that explore qualitative inner expression, such as music, dance, drama, literature, social studies, religion, personal relationships and service to the community, are fitted into any remaining time. Yet, in this latter group of subjects are the very ones that educate our choices; how we decide relationships and our life paths. These are the qualitative tools we should use to select from the vast array of scientific possibility to decide the kind of world we wish to live in. They determine our discrimination, and hence our confidence to make such informed personal choices, from which we co-create our world. The present emphasis of the school curriculum is the opposite of informed co-creation. It is no more than a training to concentrate minds and capacities to push and shove in an amoral rat race to consume the world to global destruction. Discrimination is cast aside in favour of what will be most immediately effective.

Science and education for better lives
The *Golden Standard* requires this mechanistic emphasis in education to be reversed. The core of a society's education is initiation into that society's mores. What we teach the growing generation will become their motivational heart as adults. If we teach amoral competition, our world can be no more than this. If we teach understanding, we will seek to find it in our dealings with each other. So, human, creative, cultural and religious values and personal development subjects should be the vital core.

Also, education needs to take account of who is learning and not just of what must be learnt. Focusing on the mastery of a functional curriculum, rather than the intrinsic nature of the pupils who have to master it, takes little account of their differences. It ignores not only where they are likely to succeed but also when they are likely to be ready to do so. By testing everyone against the same criteria, we dumb down the range and quality of the educational experience. Current psychological tools tend to be statistical studies, seeking to motivate pupils by grouping them in types. Leaving room for individual pupils' natures and needs does not have to be as time-consuming, as it at first seems. Very often it is much more productive.

Using astrology in schools could be a real help for teachers and pupils. Each class year will have just one or two Jupiter signs and will respond to opportunity accordingly. Taking account of the Saturn sign that changes every two to three years will be a great help in disciplining and structuring students' learning.[42] Teachers who understand astrology find that knowing a student's full birth chart can transform their relationship for the better—often solving substantial disciplinary issues.

Broadening and refocusing the curriculum to relate it more appropriately to pupils and their groups would not denigrate but enhance the learning of more functional knowledge. For, organised in this way, ultimately the qualitative aspects of the curriculum would give quantitative subjects relevance and hence meaning and purpose. Maths, science and functional English would become easier to teach and be embraced by the pupils.

Coming to adulthood, having been educated in this way, new generations will not be busy bees, with little time or confidence to do more than submit to the advice of 'properly qualified experts'. They will insist on the freedom to look deeply into the common-sense principles that should guide informed choice, not just the latest statistical study cited to ensure no one can be blamed if they 'get it wrong'. Decisions will be made with concern for people, not systems, special interests, rules and regulations. We will have the wisdom and courage to consider perspectives and views from far outside our experience and so develop the *Golden Standard* ever further in our dealings with our society and the world.

Restoring freedom to 'free enterprise'
In feudal times, the people accepted they were subject to divine providence, as passed down by the priests, empowered God and the temporal power of their 'divinely appointed' monarch and his noble lord. The Reformation, accelerated by the Enlightenment, brought the notion that every man and woman should determine their own destiny; in theory, at least! In an increasingly secular environment, the role of established religions has been replaced by

alternative ways to achieve fairer social organisation. Trades unions, welfare spending, even state ownership have been tried. Yet, the one that seems to have prevailed is, on the face of it, capable of being the most unjust – free enterprise.

Free enterprise succeeds because it sets each individual free to express and earn a living by his creative ingenuity. Everyone has a chance to achieve by doing their best. As well as making free individuals happy, such a system benefits society by allowing the combined talents of all its citizens to contribute to a richly varied open environment.

Free enterprise for whom?
Unfortunately, as we have seen in Chapters 1 and 2, free enterprise has not worked that way for the past 300+ years. Injustice comes, because, in today's world, the chance to express free creative ingenuity is enjoyed by an ever-smaller minority. Nor is the system efficient because, as we saw in Chapters 5 and 6, this small minority is less interested in creative innovation than in manipulating the people and workforce for increasingly profitable market dominance. Instead of being a free market, today's economy is run for mutual benefit by an insider group.

Just about everything done in the world economy today has little to do with the creation of a *Golden Standard* of behaviour. Quite the opposite! The pursuit of profit is considered the 'moral high ground' in international trade. Strategies to work around national business rules and procedures are devised. The rules and conditions of agreements are avoided if possible. 'We would be failing in our duty to our shareholders to act otherwise.' Lacking legal understanding or an army to support them, ordinary people suffer the consequences. Daily, their power is reduced, as it becomes concentrated in ever fewer hands.

In seeking to establish a *Golden Standard* in today's immoral economic maelstrom of greed, ignorance and hatred, the first myth to put to rest is that it has to be this way, because people are naturally cruel, dishonest and greedy. The 'harsh reality of the world and nature as it is', means the global race is the only way modern business can be conducted. To think this way is a radical incompetent error on the road to the suffering of constant crisis! How we do business today is not practical, realistic or sustainable. We are more like a hungry horde breaking through into a place of plenty and gorging ourselves to death, while the strongest among us gather and guard ever greater piles.

Astro-cycles indicate growth-based capitalism's endgame
When the astro-cycles are easy and vast areas of the world remain untapped, the consequences of such self-serving greed can be absorbed. Today, resources are increasingly limited and the astro-cycles require uncompromising honesty and efficiency. The notion that growth rate should be the unquestioned measure of economic success or failure is neither honest, nor efficient, and certainly not scientific. Like 'profit', it is an arbitrarily conceived desire concept. Neither can be scientific, because they ask more questions than they answer. What caused the growth or profit? Who experienced it, at whose expense? Is it sustainable? How much happiness has been created?

The triple conjunction of Saturn joining Pluto in Capricorn from late 2017 will demand uncompromising answers to these questions – especially when Jupiter is there from December 2019 into 2020. Some of the triple conjunction interactions have not come together like this for 5,000 years.

Little of the modern world remains untapped. The reins of military power are in the hands of vastly different cultures, driven by conflicting beliefs. If each group, culture and country applies the intransigent Capricorn conjunction with uncompromising self-interest, not only economic but internal and international violence could build to horrific experiences. There will be nowhere to hide away and defend what we value and wish to continue to have.

We save ourselves from all this by realising that narrow self-interest is never the answer. On the contrary, this decade's remaining astro-transits suggest it will be the very cause of the fearful things we are so desperate to avoid. Sharing what we have is the answer; not fighting for more and more in fear of losing what we have. Celebrating their advantage over others is how insecure cowards create enemies. The courageous do not to rush to judge and protect, but seek to understand and accommodate the needs of strangers. The truly courageous make those strangers friends; far more beneficial to move over, make room, bring more and more people with them.

If we are wise in the next few years, our descendants in the decades and centuries ahead will thank the Pluto-in-Capricorn period because, at last, it contained the force to undermine and make us reject the growth-obsessed, monetarist world economy. Forcing that intrinsically corrupt system to its endgame, even risking global disorder, did not destroy what we had, but opened a door that encouraged the search for a better, humanitarian basis to our relationships with each other.

Aquarian answers?
After the triple conjunction in Capricorn, Jupiter and Saturn move on to conjunct each other in the first degree of Aquarius on the 2020 Winter Solstice[43]. Pluto stays behind, not reaching there until January 2024. Does this mean that 'things will get better'?

Not that simple! Pluto transits are never easy and Aquarian planets have an arrogant, intolerant 'I know better than you' side, as we saw with the attitude of politicians, mechanistic scientists and financiers between 1998 and 2010, when Uranus and Neptune were either in, or mutually receiving each other, in Aquarius and Pisces. Then clever minds focused Aquarian-Piscean ingenuity upon personal and sub-group gain by avoiding or manipulating rules to perpetuate a bankrupt economy. During this time, those holding the reins of economic and political power used rules as weapons to dispossess the weak and vulnerable. This breaking and misuse of rules became the root causes of cynicism, conflict and crime; even international terrorism.

We will have until Pluto's 2043 Piscean ingress to do much better than this; to transform those early-century actions and turn our world into a much kinder and more humane expression of Aquarius.

To avoid a meltdown in the fabric of the planet and brutal conflict between its peoples as they struggle for survival, we must use our brilliance, not to beat and defeat, but to support each other. Scientific brilliance should turn away from energy-intense inventions to the creation of energy-efficient machines; processes that do more with less. These should reduce the working day, leaving more time for recreation with family and friends. Acquisition of money and material possessions should not be the measure of success or failure, but relegated to a role that supports our more important social lives. The financial markets must become our servants, not our masters. No longer should they be trusted as the institutions of first resort to receive, control and distribute economic resources. Their way to easy money cut off, those who continue to be obsessed with piling it up should not be rewarded. They should be regarded as objects of pity rather than envy.

The highest Aquarian humanitarian principles will be needed to underpin all final judgements on these re-ordered priorities.

Free enterprise for all
The practical, truly businesslike way is to cooperate, to support and open doors to individual enterprise. Large organisations should find it more and more difficult to

dominate. Instead, principles of fair play that favour newcomers should be established and apply all over the world. The time limits and scope of patents for new ideas, especially for large companies, should be reduced. Workers should share these rights.

We need to turn away from the notion (and the legal assumptions that come with it) that profit, whatever the consequences, is the absolute virtue of all free enterprise activity. We saw earlier that it is far from being the scientific measure of efficiency that monetarist economic theory seems to assume. It might be if every practical and ethical consideration affecting everyone is factored in. Without all this, it is an arbitrary concept of desire, attachment to which leads to temporary happiness for a few and ongoing unhappiness for the rest.

The highest and most efficient principle, for which all seeking happiness will strive, is to live a fruitful life in an increasingly cared-for world. How can we do that when the main players in our economy are pretenders, exploiters and profiteers; admired and rewarded for their wealth? As the vital importance of this question sinks in, many such people will be identified and rejected; as are the leaders of lynch mobs when reasonable law and order is restored.

This is how it should be. All negotiations must be undertaken with the motivation of wanting everyone to succeed and have what they need. Agreements should be made with the intention that all parties will fully implement them. Recognising, stating and keeping to the principles intrinsic to the agreement should be paramount: the key to the resolution of all disputes.

Such an attitude should dominate the way we relate to the world and expect it to be. The trust that comes from recognising fellow negotiators who share these values will enable sensible planning to manage astro-cycles effectively, reducing the suffering that comes from surprise and sudden loss. From such trust will develop recognition of the common humanity we share, and so a kinder, happier and, crucially, more sustainable world.

A political process all can embrace
When principle, good will and comfortable family life replace regulation, the battle for profit, and manipulation to satisfy the system's dictates, the heart of our political experience will be very different. Our institutions will enable and encourage communication across sub-cultures, by adopting the highest ethical production standards and ways to share resources. They will support those in need, care more about self-expression than self-interest, extend opportunities to contribute, celebrate and play. Once the key principles of the way we relate in society are established, politics will not be a battle between those who have and have not, but rather the way we report information and share resources. Focus groups will morph into becoming co-creators of society. For, with principle agreed, political organisation will come from local groups up to national organisation, not imposed from on high by rigorously controlled national parties. We will not be seeking ways to manipulate the money supply and other resources. Rather we will be cooperating to live within our means and care for the environment. The 'government of the people, by the people, for the people', genuinely will start to be with us here on the Earth.[44]

Real communications
So, no longer the proud posturing and egocentric greed of those who seek to fix and direct society to its way of personal profit, but the real ways and wishes of the people will take over. People will emerge from the frenetic, automative, busy yet half-aware world in which they have allowed themselves to be trapped. They will realise how they have been like moths struggling against a window

pane, seeking to force themselves toward a world into which they do not know the way.

With that barrier gone, the range and depth of the news will broaden. Background focus will show us the real reasons behind events. All perspectives will be considered, especially any individuals or groups said to be in the wrong. We will be less keen to condemn, more interested in seeking to understand the cause. Was the behaviour totally unreasonable? Knowing the whole picture will help to heal situations far more quickly and fully.

The manipulative lies of the marketing industry exposed, vast areas of media channels and many facile advertisement hoardings will change to genuine creative contributions to our lives. The room this leaves to inform what we use, consume and do will bring joyous space; room to be what we are.

Entertainment, art and sport will be just that, something to enjoy, create and share together; free of interruptions 'from our sponsors'. Commercial sponsorship may remain, but discreetly in the background, not filling every moment, giving the viewer little or no time to breathe and reflect on what has just happened.

Yes, it is possible, when we refuse to accept those 'free' commercial offers that then constantly invade, restrict and twist our lives.

Can you see that at last we are beginning to live life as we wish? Lives that we and our associates have always wanted can now start to happen?

Chapter 10
Using Astrology to Answer Our Problems

It is easy to be with some people and awkward with others. So, does that mean it is best to identify and stay with those friends and experiences we are most comfortable with? Surely, the most skilful way to lead a happy life is to focus on our interests and stay away from distracting people and activities?

Paradoxically, narrowing our lives in this way is the gateway to misunderstanding and dissatisfaction. People who are like us still seem to compete or have foibles that annoy. Being with soulmates can shut out the rest of the world. Each other's delusions can be confirmed. We develop 'them and us' attitudes and become paranoid.

On the other hand, what can we do when we feel ignored and misunderstood, or find that how people act is infuriating? The answer lies in understanding karma as the cause of differences between people and events. From this, we develop tolerant discrimination and make the best use of what at first may seem alien. The proper use of astrology is an invaluable support in doing this.

We start by accepting that our mind, our mental attitude towards phenomena, is the creator of all our experiences. Although the nature and actions of other people may trigger our experiences, it is our mental dispositions, dependent upon our own previous actions and developed perceptions, that create those experiences. So, the first step in understanding and clearing the problem is to step outside ourselves and examine our own perceptions. Astrology is an objective tool to assist us in this. The earlier books in this Astrological Quartet series gives us the astrological language to see and come to respect, even enjoy, the differences between ourselves and others. It opens doors to, and allows us to feel secure in, worlds we would hesitate otherwise to

Using Astrology to Answer Our Problems 139

enter. It helps us to be comfortable with people we would avoid, if we did not have the astro-information about where we both stand in terms of each other.

Of course, we do not need to know astrology to do this. Through patient maturity, even simple good breeding, people come to tolerate and make allowances for others. The wise know that opposites attract and familiarity can breed contempt. There are many psychological analyses and procedures that categorise and advise on 'how to make friends and influence people'. Yet, few systems have the potential to know, accept and celebrate people for what they are better than astrology. This is best illustrated by example. This chapter will conclude by illustrating this with a deep study of one of today's key world problems. To feel our way in, let us start with a lighter example: the astrology of the relationship between the comedy duo Laurel and Hardy!

The astrology of the Laurel and Hardy relationship

This comedy duo dominated the 1920-40s silent and early sound cinema screens. Although their mutual personal chemistry was distinctively their own, many of its elements seem to have inspired comedy duos through the decades to the present day.

The uniqueness of this personal chemistry is clear from their birth charts. With Jupiter in Pisces rising and ruling both his first and public 10th houses, Oliver Hardy was clearly the obese one and a natural victim. Yet the Sun and Mercury in Capricorn meant he always saw himself as being in control. Saturn in the 7th house of relationships in early Libra indicates that it was his constant struggle to 'take charge' and hang on to this control, while Stan and others always seemed to let him down. The Moon there too in Virgo opposed to Jupiter suggests that obsessively critical attention to detail exacerbated such victim situations. Mars in Scorpio in the 9th squared Venus in Aquarius in the 12th, suggests his effectiveness was undermined by needing to help everyone.

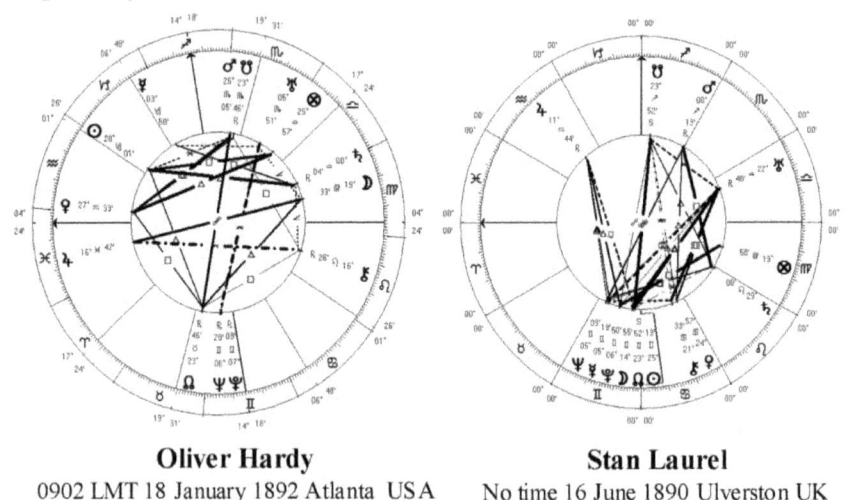

Oliver Hardy
0902 LMT 18 January 1892 Atlanta USA

Stan Laurel
No time 16 June 1890 Ulverston UK

Although we do not have the time of birth to orientate Stan Laurel's chart, wherever his stellium in Gemini lies, it certainly suggests a terrible aggravation to Oliver Hardy's 3rd house of communication. Nothing irritates Capricorns more than distracting ideas that prevent the job being completed correctly. Even worse is that, with so much Gemini, Stan will seem to accept what Oliver insists upon instantly, but then change approach or do something entirely different. With such an inventive mind, Stan's scripts for the comedy routines often turned around who was responsible for the 'fine mess' they got into. The audience could see that Oliver's carefully controlled way of doing something was doomed from the start. However much Stan's Gemini tried to correct the situation they were in, it only made matters worse.

Stan's Mars retrograding back across the Sagittarius-Scorpio cusp to square Saturn at the end of Leo suggests constant problems of identity. That his Mars is moving to meet Oliver's in late Scorpio is a key astro-factor that brought this disparate pair to act together. There is slickness to Mars in Scorpio, which it rules. This is a key to the way the men appear to bumble through one disaster after another with a keen underlying sense of comic timing. Oliver's Mars in the 9th suggests international recognition that was to last long beyond their time in the limelight.

We do not know if the two men knew about, let alone used, astrology. It is more likely that they had the maturity, tolerance and intelligence to step back from attachment to their very different natures, and so liberate the ludicrousness of their trying to work together, turning it into celebrated comedy entertainment. Clearly Stan and Oliver were exceptional human beings, who could look at themselves objectively and see the nonsensical humour of the way they were, both individually and together. Then, rather than reject and go their separate ways, they used their birth karma positively to transform their lives and entertain millions for decades.

The astrology of everyone's relationship
By studying the astrology of the above relationship, we can see that astrology is a language of understanding that anyone can use to put their lives and relationships in perspective. It helps us to step outside ourselves, to avoid blaming others for being different. No longer are we uncomfortable, even defensive, when meeting strangers.

Using astrology this way offers a far more positive and creative way of living our lives. More examples will make this clear. Mars rules both Aries and Scorpio. Both crave action, but very different kinds of action. Being a fire sign, Aries action needs to be immediate, rough and even raw. Arians are pioneers breaking new territory. Scorpio, being a water sign, want to *feel* the full effect of what is done — to experience it 'hitting the spot'. Scorpios rest in the dark mysteriousness of sexuality and renewal. From these key distinctions it is clear why people with planets focused in these signs might feel uncomfortable with, even threatened by, each other. By knowing their astrology and hence how they tick, each will relate more easily and see mutual benefit in each other's qualities.

Taurus and Libra are both ruled by Venus. Both seek love and creativity. Being an earth sign, Taureans hold on to and develop material possessions through ownership, business, gardening, farming, pottery. Librans, being an air sign, focus their love into keeping relationships balanced. They seek ideas that bring peace between people. They fear instability, losing control. Taureans may offer Librans firmness and the materials to resource their endeavours, while Librans have the tools to negotiate the proper distribution of those resources.

The meanings and associations in *The Secret Language of Astrology* offer a rich source of concepts to compare and methods to synthesise them in a wide variety of ways. With them it is much easier to know where you stand, appreciate and work with anyone. For proper astrology is much more than the Sun or even planets in signs. It interprets angular connections between them and the orientation of the Earth on its axis. It looks at all these factors at the time of birth and then compares them to the new celestial positions at moments of future time.

This has profound implications for those who see meaning beyond ordinary material concerns; especially if they believe the karmic consequences of our actions go forward over more than one lifetime. My *Astrology and*

Compassion the Convenient Truth explains the Tibetan view of reincarnation that the state of mind at the time of death grasps to find a new incarnation to continue to work out its past-life karma. If the astrological patterns in the heavens at the time of birth indicate the individual nature, then the karmic residue at the death of that lifetime will be drawn to reincarnate, to be born at a new fitting birth point of time and space. From then the new life must come to terms with past-life karma. The planetary transits of the new lifetime show the new challenges we will confront through it.

Institutions, nations and historical movements follow similar karmic processes, with natures that can be explained and clarified by using astro-cycles. The section below shows how astrology can be used to explain and start to cut through the causes and cures to one of the most intractable problems the world faces today.

Answering world problems
Most of us are emotionally stirred and find ourselves applauding to the rooftops when one of our pet injustices is publicly identified. Yet how many of us sustain the same enthusiasm when asked to pay the price to put it right? Instead, we flounder around seeking other people ('far guiltier than we') to transfer the blame to. We insist they fulfil our idealism by paying to put our principles into place. Unfortunately, however, those in need must accept that their wishes are not possible for everyone in the 'real world'.

This is the nub of the problem. Thinking and acting in the ways listed below show we do not have the courage and human kindness to go that extra mile to find real solutions.

- ❖ No child should drown on an alien shore, but we do not have room for any more immigrants in our town (unless they work in our health service).
- ❖ Supplying arms to terrorists and corrupt regimes leads to terrible suffering and danger to innocent people. Nuclear

weapons place a meaningless financial burden on our economy, but under no circumstances should the jobs of our country's arms workers be threatened.
- ❖ We blame bankers for exploiting and misleading us, but weakly use their system and let them blackmail us with their remuneration demands.
- ❖ We welcome foreign property investment, even if this prices normal residents out of their cities.

The result of these and our many other shortcomings leads to the worst of all worlds, where we fester in a maelstrom of basic ignorance, resentment and guilt. This way we are all the root cause of the ongoing suffering that haunts our world.

The astrology of the perpetuation of suffering

Underpinned by such fragments of lethal inconsistency, long-standing errors of attitude cause ongoing global suffering. Great historical religious-social fault lines are perpetuated by separate cultures and religions initiating each new generation into remembering and seeking retribution for atrocities dating back centuries, even millennia. So poignantly expressed in Shakespeare's *Romeo and Juliet*: great tragedy comes from assuming it is unthinkable to see from a perceived enemy's point of view and resolve long-standing disputes.

The Middle East crisis touches many areas of many lives in our world today. It emanates from the angst of three key long-standing historical disputes between or within three of the world's key religious cultures: The Crucifixion of Jesus Christ; the Roman destruction of the Jewish temple; and the dispute over the successor to the Prophet, that led to Islam's schism into the Shia and Sunni traditions. Today, conflict over these spills over into threatening the safety of people throughout the world. Astrology can help us understand the heart errors that led to such

Using Astrology to Answer Our Problems 145

misunderstanding, and so empathise with the feelings of all sides involved.

The destruction of the Jewish temple

To understand the Jewish side of the story, we need to go back to the early Christian Era,[45] to the destruction of the Jewish temple by the Romans in 70 CE.

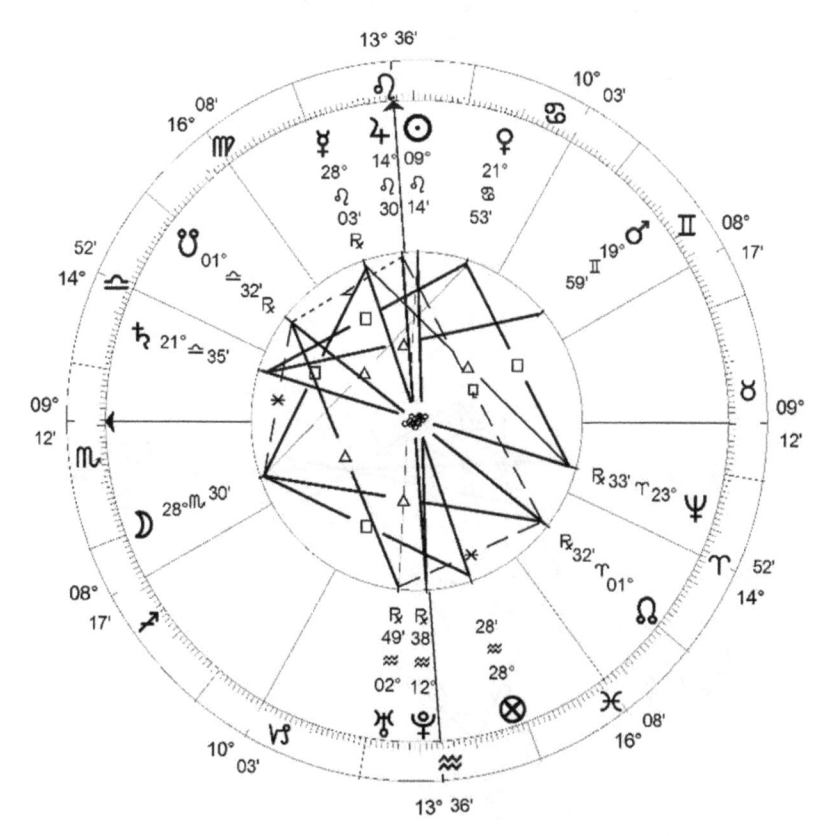

Destruction of Jewish Temple
Noon LMT 4 August 0070 Jerusalem, Israel

Put yourself in the place of the Jewish people that day, confronted by an arrogant Roman imperial power (Sun-Jupiter-Mercury in Leo) determined to destroy the very basis of your culture (opposed Pluto in Aquarius). Imagine the hurt and horror of others denying everything you believe in and place all your reliance upon (T-square between Neptune in Aries, Venus in Cancer and Saturn in Libra). How much resentment would this experience trigger and become enshrined into the future against anyone you need to defend yourself from (Moon in Scorpio squared Mercury in Leo)? The only way to survive as a race would seem to be to hold, sustain and perpetuate the values of your people against any who seek to deny them; keep your distance, do not totally integrate, and so pass down the memory of this moment from generation to generation (Moon in Scorpio grand trine North Node in Aries and Venus in Cancer).

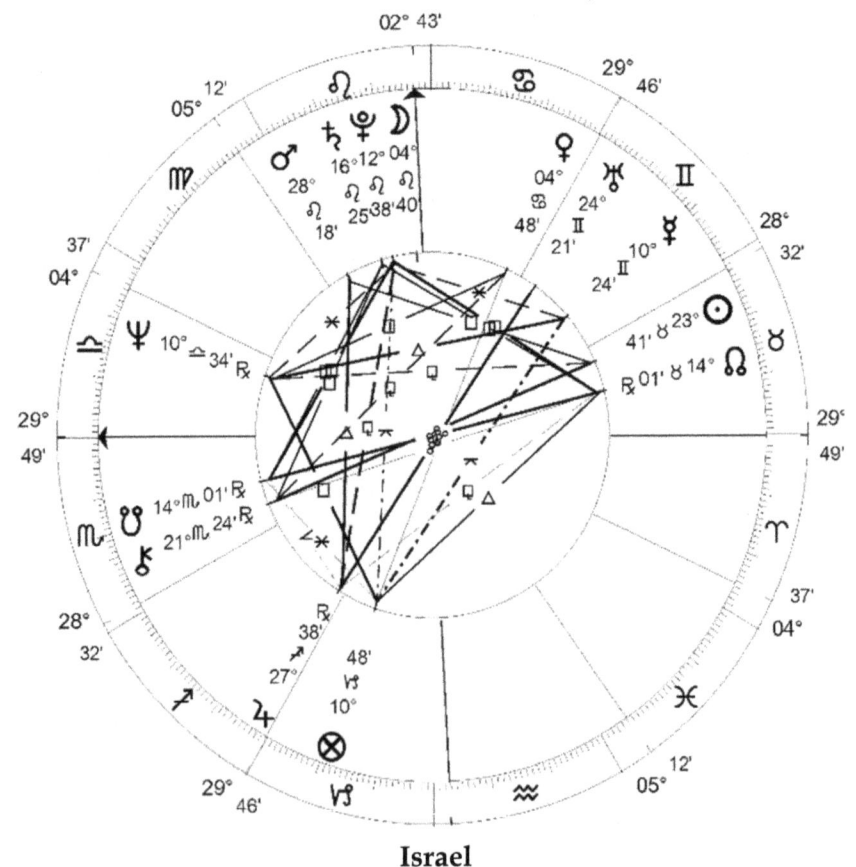

Israel
1632 EET 14th May 1948 Jerusalem Israel

In this way, these outcast people sustained their culture for millennia, until the horrors of World War Two created

Using Astrology to Answer Our Problems 147

momentum that opened a window of opportunity, which in 1948 to return to their 'Promised land'. Near two thousand years of remembering and yearning packed them with determination to defend and grow from this opportunity. Comparing the Destruction of the Temple chart to the one for the birth of modern Israel shows that Israelis would be as proud and uncompromising in defending their nation as had been the Romans in taking it away (Moon, Pluto [in almost exact opposition to its position at the destruction], Saturn and Mars in Leo [conjunct the destruction Mercury]).

The Middle East Mandate
However, much had happened during the Jewish exile from Palestine. It had become home to a mainly Muslim indigenous population for more than one thousand years

After the mutual slaughter of the medieval Crusades, Eastern European countries struggled to contain the Ottoman Empire. For much of this time, Shia and Sunni Muslims lived with each other through the Middle East.

Following the defeat and break-up of the previously ruling Ottoman Empire, the post-World-War-One arrangements (mainly by Britain and France),[46] arbitrarily created kingdoms that cut across cultures and religions. This misunderstanding of traditions and their issues lit fires of conflict, which today seem to be blazing out of control.

Astrology could have warned the Middle East Mandate conference delegates. The chart on page 146 shows their chosen meeting clearly indicated a time for badly thought out decisions that would lead to conflict (Mercury in Aries trine Moon, Neptune and Jupiter in Leo, all three exactly conjunct on the day). So it was in Syria that by favouring the minority Alawite Shia people, the French mandate sowed the seeds for today's conflict. In Iraq, in an attempt to impose unwanted unity, the British were the first to consider using their mandate to be the first to consider dropping gas on the Kurds. When implementing its Palestine protectorate,

Britain implemented Balfour's well intentioned 1917 Accord to allow in and seek to integrate Jewish immigrants with the resident Palestinians. The situation was made impossible by the exodus following the World War Two Holocaust. The United States supported the UN recognition of Israel, which declared itself a state (Sun in Taurus in the 1920 Mandate Chart and the Israel birth chart).

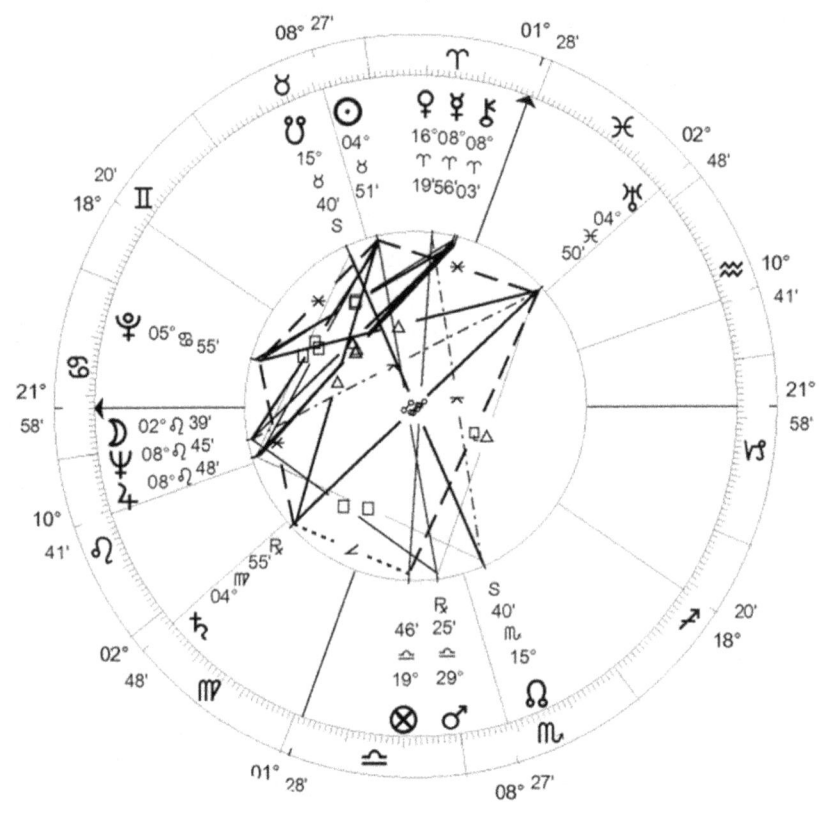

Middle East Mandate
1122 CEDT 25 April 1920 San Remo, Italy

The dire consequences directly and indirectly resulting from the establishment of the State of Israel are well known. So, now put yourself in the position of a Palestinian, chased from your family home by decisions agreed and materially supported by strange religious cultures living thousands of miles away. Indigenous Palestinians saw the Jewish newcomers as usurpers, bringing destruction and unending hurt and suffering. No wonder then that the charts for the consequent escalations of conflict the years that followed have numerous astro-connections to the earlier Temple, Israel and Middle East Mandate charts.

The astrology of a missed opportunity

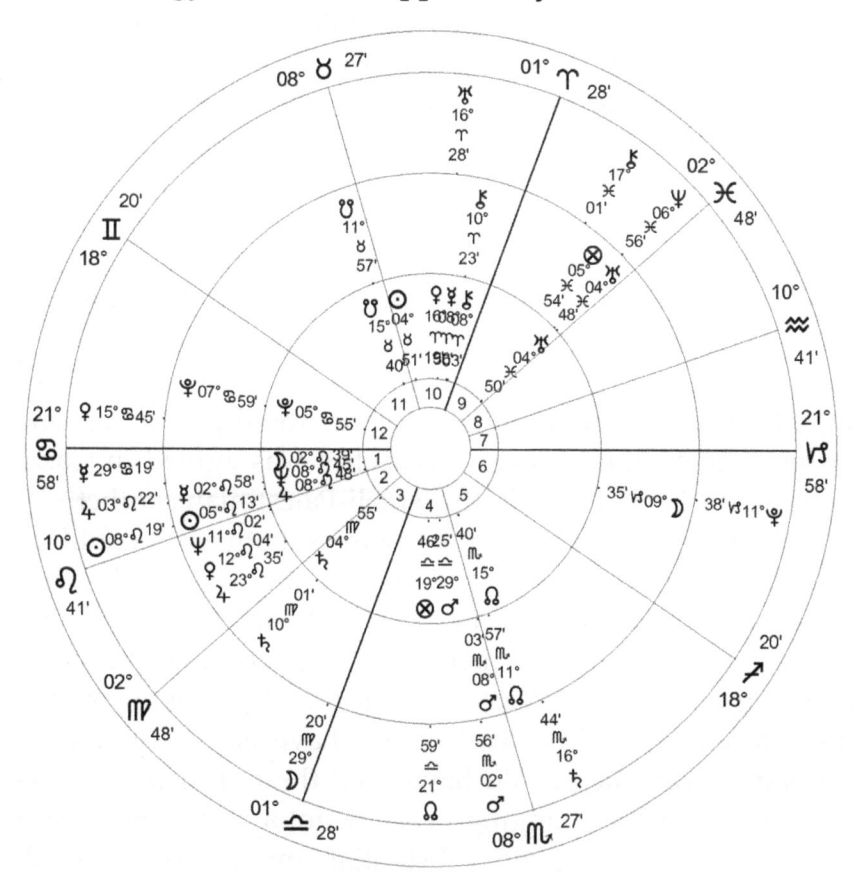

Middle East Mandate
Progressions & Transits to 31 July 2014

Even when astro-events indicate the possibility of peace, it seems resentment, the taste for revenge, or the fear of losing control is so entrenched that no more than a shift from full bloody destruction to an uneasy ceasefire is possible.

The July-August 2014 Gaza War is just one of many violent flare-ups in the ongoing conflict between Israel and the Palestinians. As in past conflicts, its progress can be traced in the progressions and transits to the 1920 Middle East Mandate chart. Resentment was fuelled and resources built up by transiting Saturn squaring the Leo stellium in the natal and progressed charts through the preceding months. It was triggered into active conflict when Mars squared the natal Moon, conjuncted by progressed Mercury, in late July and continued to square natal Neptune-Jupiter and progressed Sun-Neptune-Venus, as the violence intensified.

However, the fighting ended before Mars squared the progressed Jupiter. The great French astrologer André Barbault has made a thorough study[47] of beneficent Venus-Jupiter conjunctions, showing how frequently they coincide with armistice and ceasefire agreements, especially when these connect with key parts of the chart. So, in August 2014 with transiting Venus-Jupiter conjunct the Jupiter- Neptune of the 1920 Mandate chart, a ceasefire was agreed in Gaza, pausing the latest phase in the Israeli-Palestinian conflict.

By labelling each other as enemies, both sides could do no more than react automatically to the astro-cycles and aggravate rather than placate. They left each other churning in ever more resentment, merely adding another sad chapter to the thousands of years of tragedy. By looking at the transits ahead of time, both could have acted differently. Instead of war, they could have used these difficult transits to go through life-changing peace negotiations, where both sides would have given substantial amounts of ground. Then that rare Venus-Jupiter transit in Leo would have marked more than a temporary respite to boiling resentment, seeking ever more terrible ways to wreak revenge. It could have bought a genuine long-term breakthrough: a relieving peace for all.

Using Astrology to Answer Our Problems 151

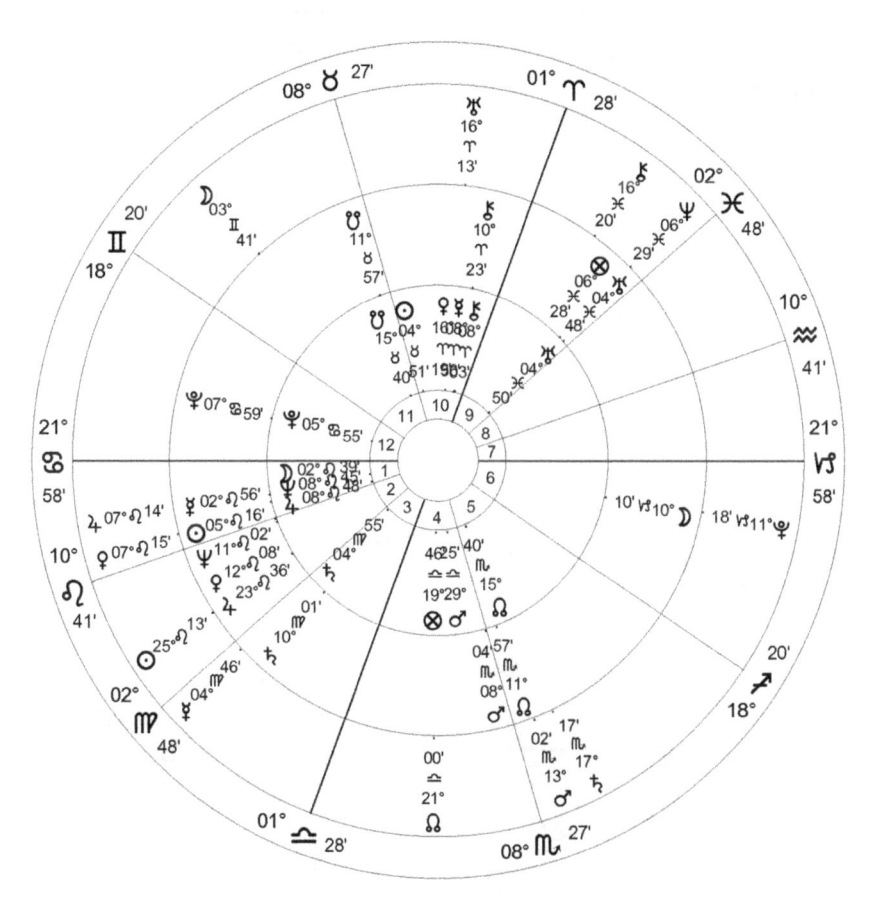

Middle East Mandate
Progressions & Transits to 18 August 2014

Isil - the endgame of revenge

So, time and time again, brutal knee-jerk decisions followed by missed opportunities for peace have driven the ongoing tragedy. Mindlessly, we react to the transiting planets and their connections to the charts of earlier key moments.

The US invasion of Iraq, in reaction to the 9-11 atrocity in New York, triggered a dire worsening of Middle East relationships, both with the west and within the area. What happened then, and the attempts by both the Bush and Obama administrations to build western-style democracy there, dominate today's decisions. Constant threats cast a shadow upon people's lives throughout the planet. How did it come to this?

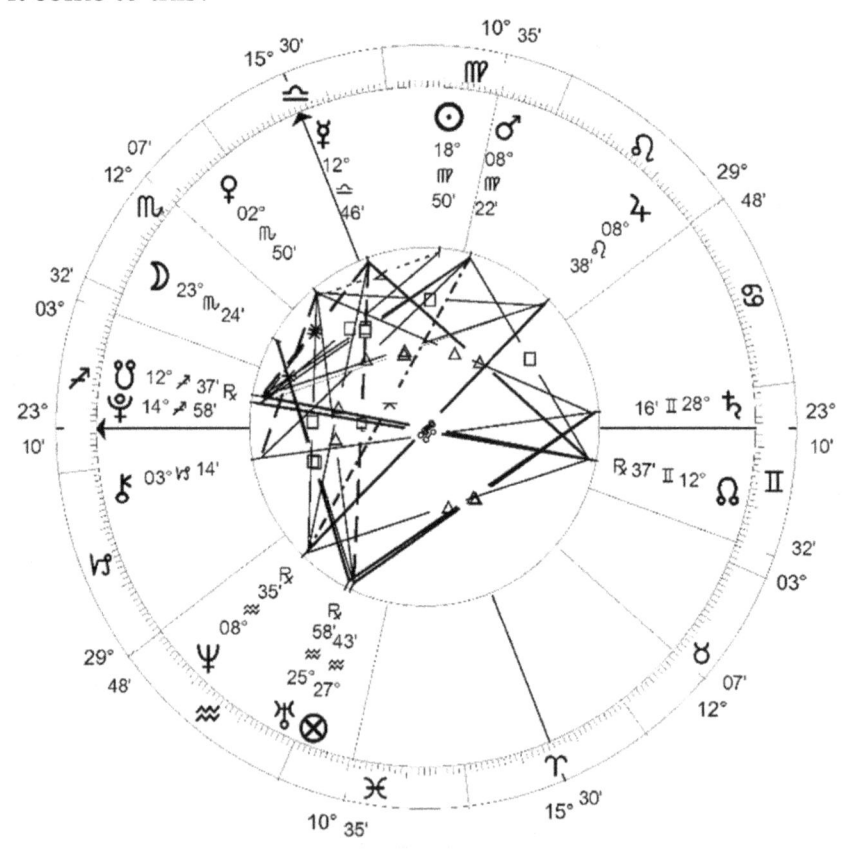

World Leaders at Ground Zero
1430 EDT 11 September 2002 New York US

The first Solar Return chart of the event clearly shows a trap that no wise, astro-cycle-aware policy maker would fall into. To the day one year after the 9-11 atrocity, Jupiter and Neptune made an exact opposition, with transiting Jupiter less than a degree from the degree of their exact 1920 conjunction. Transiting Neptune was opposed that degree.

Clearly unaware that their own charts were dangerously connected to this opposition,[48] George W Bush and Tony Blair became mindlessly consumed by the transit. They believed they could impose beneficial western ways of government upon a culture and history they did not understand. Concocting reasons to invade Iraq with 'shock and awe', they further destabilised the region.

The dark ethos of what we now know as Isil, IS or Daesh emerged under various other names from the late 1990s. *The Washington Post* shows clearly how much of its expansion into an effective fighting force, under the name of the Islamic State of Syria and the Levant [Isil], grew out of links made in Camp Bucca, an American prison in Iraq.[49] Chaotic resentment at the disbanding and imprisonment of Saddam's Ba'athParty members was a major factor.

At Isil's 2013 formal announcement of its role beyond Syria, it specifically committed itself to the destruction of the Sykes-Picot protocol,[50] upon which the 1920 Mandate agreement was founded. The Isil April 2013 foundation chart has many Aries planets near key Mandate chart degrees.

The impulsive ignorance of this post World War One agreement reinforced the ghostly distant memory of the medieval Crusades. The West's creation and support of Israel, followed by a whole series of clumsy interventions, all together have played into the hands of those intent on death-dealing extremism. So now the whole world faces a seemingly irreconcilable cultural schism between two diametrically opposite moralities.

In Daesh territories, a woman who shows any part of her body is severely punished. On the beach in France, it is crime for her to swim with too many clothes on! There, women are expected to show most, but not quite all, of their bodies. western morality celebrates this life's indulgent possessions of the flesh. Displays of sexuality titillate and drive our economy.

Isil seeks to convert, on pain of death, all other Muslim groups and unbelievers alike to accept their 'pure and beautiful heaven', reached by a strict literal interpretation of Sharia Law. To convert the world to its ways, it commits, and encourages the committing of, atrocities that aim to turn societies against Islam absolutely, thinking this will bring more and more Muslims into its fold.

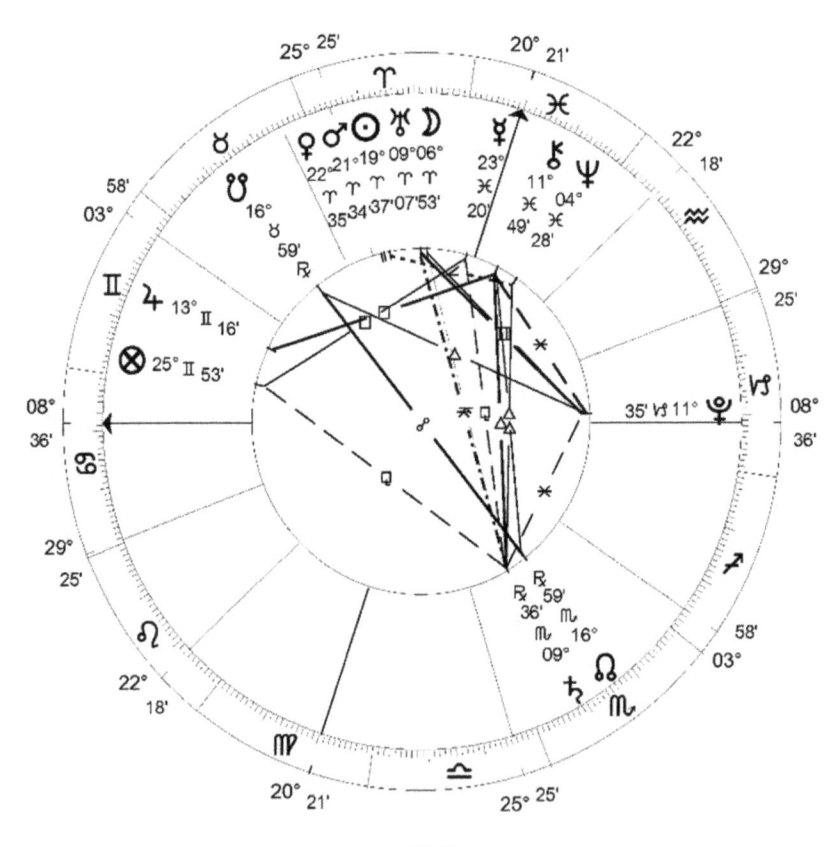

ISIL
1045 EEDT 9 April 2013 Aleppo Syria

Myriad ways of revenge following revenge have brought us to this. Revenge creates new causes of bitterness that raise the stakes and consequent suffering higher and higher. Murder and 'death to the murderers' seems to be the only way ahead. Not knowing any better, without astrology's wiser means of objective assessment, national leaders and their people refuse to let go of their myopic self-centred views.

Not looking at situations through other people's eyes, each side fails to realise there is no such thing as 'righteous payback'; just the unbearable pain it continually creates. So, by basing action on the diametrically opposed rules of each sub-group, all feel they must commit ever more horrific acts of barbarity. Moving ever further apart and full of desperate bitterness, finally, all that remains is uncompromising darkness, demanding we surrender absolutely to the very opposite of all we believe in, or die.

Solving problems by looking through others' eyes
The first vital thing to realise is that nothing, however terrible and unforgivable, happens without a prior cause, and that cause can go back a long way and land in some unexpected places.

To find this cause, we just must look deep and far enough from our own selfish interest. When we do, we will see that people behave badly when they are treated badly. Hence, to start putting right a problem, we must stop behaving badly toward each other. Provided we are willing to ask: 'What have we done to create the situation?' it never will be too late to put it right; however bad it seems to be.

Armed with the humility of a selfless answer, the next vital step is to stop making matters worse. In the current tense, social climate, the French banning the wearing of the burka, or even the burkini when swimming, will alienate many who would prefer to be friends. The German open door immigration policy may lead to many difficulties of adjustment, but these can be difficulties that lead to mutual understanding.

Let us state it again! Peaceful resolution of conflict becomes possible when, while continuing to honour our own cultural tradition, we try to see the world from the perspective of those we previously assumed were our enemies. What follows are attempts to do just that.

❖ In the late 1940s, the fate of the Jewish people turned around dramatically. Having narrowly avoided racial obliteration, they could return to their Promised Land after two thousand years of exile, persecution and marginalisation.

Triumphant relief fired determination first to defend, and then build, their new national homeland. Armed with the good will and support of many nations, they were faced with the Palestinian population, with a very different thousands-of-years cultural history.

Jewish immigrants, mostly from European cultures, trying to establish an uneasy foothold in an unfamiliar land, were suspicious of the intentions of the indigenous people. They naturally turned to those who had established themselves under the British Mandate and the ex-terrorist groups, who had fought against the British.

What happened consequently has savagely soured the mutual respect and cooperation between the two peoples and explains the insecurity that seems to hang endlessly over the future of Israel. It has darkened the world standing of the US, Israel's chief political and military supporter, ever since. This in turn has emboldened Israeli policies of expansion into the West Bank. Islamic fanatics exploit the sense of injustice to justify the direst acts of terror, spreading way beyond Israel, Palestine and the Middle East.

Now see through Israeli eyes. From the beginning, they were there, but not wanted and attacked at every stage. As a consequence, ordinary people were increasingly torn apart by extremism. On one hand the most extreme Zionists, urging the absolute righteousness of an exclusively Jewish Palestine, against on the other uncompromising calls for the State of Israel to be wiped from the face of the Earth. In the middle, just as bad, are those that pretend to talk peace, merely to 'push the goal posts' ever-closer to their extreme goal.

Roots of mistrust and intolerance demonstrated here, and in all the other surrogate conflicts that have erupted in

Using Astrology to Answer Our Problems 157

the area since, undermine the whole world's ability to live in harmony. For when we have the material power to ignore and dominate, this is when we should not do so. When we feel no need to consider the interests of others, at that very time we should look into their minds and sympathise with their predicament. By any means possible, seek to resolve every battle and policy initiative. Happiness and peace come when we meet each other in a spirit of giving.

❖ Put yourself in the mind of a Palestinian householder, forced by superior force out of a home that was owned your family for centuries; to be exiled, ignored, reduced to grudging acceptance in the refugee camps of neighbouring countries. Feeling unheard and desperate, turning to terrorist acts, even suicide. Whatever you do only seems to make your oppressors stronger.

To break the pattern of this spiralling down to unbearable deprivation, can you find it in your heart to want to put aside the wrongs of the past? Like you, now the Jewish people have nowhere else to live. Would it not be better to accept, to seek ways to cooperate and co-create parallel, mutually respecting cultures. Accept generous recompense and find a way back to live with, share and then restore your people's ability to grow and prosper?

❖ Now visualise yourself as a seventh-century Muslim conqueror of the Middle East, North Africa and Spain, driven by faith in the one God, inspired by the quality of your culture, rejecting totally and sweeping aside all opposition. Are you sure this way will last forever?

Now transfer your mind to take part in the inevitable Christian backlash that followed. Become a determined medieval crusader, crossing Europe to Palestine, to the very gates of the Holy City of Jerusalem. In the name of the only righteous God, do such savage deeds so that still in the twenty-first century the word 'crusader' is used by some to characterise the 'abomination' of western society.

❖ Take on the mind of the conquering righteousness of all European colonialists, who come to 'save primitive souls' with 'holy words', concealing weapons of conquest and economic exploitation. So full of ourselves that we do not see the need to ask what could be learnt from those we enslave. So, like all such conquerors, we are doomed to rule, maybe flourish for a while, and then degenerate. In turn, to be conquered and become just one more deluded unhappy egoist in the history of delusion and misunderstanding.

The story of the British colonisation of India offers a balance of highly informative contrasting assumptions and outcomes, elegantly drawn in E M Forster's *A Passage to India*. Numerous real-life examples show that when openness to the indigenous culture led to mature understanding, the best of both worlds was possible. When it did not, prejudice and brutality seemed unavoidable.

❖ Fast forward and focus now on the libertarian behaviour patterns of our modern times. The growing sexualisation of the dress, art and entertainment in the western world over the past hundred years. Although our Victorian forebears may not have been any more moral than us in their private lives, they would have seen the public dress, painted faces and LGBT acceptance of the twenty-first century as profoundly corrupt.

The West is so far beyond such attitudes that to question a person's freedom to be this way is to deny their human rights. It could even be illegal. In contrast, consider a society where the woman is completely covered and all LGBT relationships and activities are severely punished.

Now step back from both. Provided the choices are freely made and the behaviour is motivated by good intention, is not any form of dress a mask? Do we see the real person behind a scantily dressed, heavily made-up man or woman any more than we do behind someone dressed in a full burka?

Are not all expressions of affection a search to love and be loved? Is the dismissive, exploitative, even brutal way that one culture behaves to another intrinsically different?

Rather, is it caused by confused cultural differences, tangled up with a history of bad behaviour from both sides? If we both were to let go and live in each other's cultures for a while, we would find much to learn and appreciate. This would adapt and enrich mutual understanding.

❖ In family relationships, great sustaining love is needed to endure each member's divergent natures and circumstances. There could be no greater contrast than between the total dependence of the infant and the desperate need for independence of the adolescent. Numerous book and film dramas depict parents egocentrically projecting their own shortcomings, aspirations and fears upon their offspring. Consequential fear, guilt and over-dependence or accusation, blame, rejection and even mindless rebellion result. Parental shortcomings, even abuse, can ensue; sometimes complicated by false 'recovered' memories of what never occurred. Only great love, remembering the kindness at the best of times, when amidst the worst of times is the way most families stay loyally together. As Confucius taught, such families show us the way.

How to transform suffering into happiness

Giving up what seems essential, indispensably precious to us and our loved ones, letting go of deeply felt assumptions, may feel uncomfortably dangerous. It is much easier to accept convention and hide behind what everyone tells us are the harsh realities of the world, 'as it is and always has been'. After all, when 'it comes down to it' is not 'every person or people in it for themselves'? Do not animals hunt each other for food? Would we not follow suit if we were hungry? Is it not the natural way of things for people to be selfish and greedy? Surely, only fools give up what is precious and leave themselves vulnerable, exposed to the evil greedy alien beliefs and behaviour patterns of others? Is not the struggle to dominate the root of our righteousness? This is the natural way of the world.

Quite the opposite! It is when we face and work through the threshold of difficulty to a mutually acceptable solution that *real* achievements become possible. Cross-country runners recognise the impossible pain that must be endured early in the race, just before settling into their rhythm. All athletes train ever harder to succeed. We work especially hard before exams. The writing of this book will be worked and worried over many times, until the ideas can be clear to as many people as possible. Great comedians constantly practise their routines. The best achievements in every walk of life come through determination and the courage to persist. Through faith and confidence to carry on, we clear clouds of confusion. We can then see truth, like a glorious sun, and enjoy great achievements that had long seemed impossible. Magically it becomes so, because we just could not let go of wanting it!

This requires a happy mind, ready to welcome and transform unwanted sufferings into opportunities to solve problems. Realise nothing is for ever. Trying to hold on to unavoidably changing circumstances is the root cause of most suffering. The more we fear death, betrayal or loss of possessions, the more hurt these very possessions will cause us. The solution is not to see the people that seem to threaten as enemies, but as seekers after happiness like us. In all situations, there is a middle way. Rather like tuning a radio, it is to be found by understanding, but not wanting, the extremes. Knowing this, we can find and rest comfortably at very best signal in-between.

As individuals, families, groups, societies, religions, cultures, countries and parts of the world, we must step away from the counterproductive illusory 'security' of assumed realities to the lasting security of understanding differences and working together.

Forgiving the unforgivable - unity in international affairs
In international affairs self-interest that breaks agreements and harms others must be condemned totally, not selectively. To condemn others when it suits our foreign policy objectives, and then ignore the same offence when our friends are the perpetrators, is worse than having no rules at all. Without fear or favour all offenders should be ostracised, arms supply strictly controlled, no matter how it affects the financial and policy self-interest of the supplier. Everyone must develop the deepest commitment to justice, so that an ever-expanding number of people share the same commitment to the same fundamental truth.

Projecting the blame for our unhappiness on others never solves problems. It makes them worse. As rulership by lies and brute force fades, so will the sense of unfairness that leads to conflict. As we move even-handedly towards ideal principles, the clouds of confusion will start clearing. We will see the unity of kindness and tolerance within all communities and their people. We will come to understand and accept the natural flow. We will work with its rise and fall within everyone.

Great love is needed to resolve great conflicts. There is no other way. We must cross the divide, even if marked by an iron barrier. See beyond ourselves, relax into empathy; let the sorrow out. Open windows to that harmonic oneness, which holds everything in the Universe together. Do not squander any chance of healing – learn to love. Discover and live in societies that accept unshakeable principles.

Believing such forgiveness is possible
How can we be like this, when everyone around us seems intent on personal dominance? Do they? Look deeper! Knowing what your opponent wants is certainly a good strategy in sport. It is equally so when seeking better ways to organise our lives and our planet. Most people want to do good things and live happy, friendly, interesting lives with

each other. Those living in the few remaining traditional parts of the world, still hardly touched by western ways, do not need more and more money and possessions to be happy. Rather, they seek to understand and respect every element of their natural environment and co-create with it a world that is right for themselves.

Understanding the causes of unacceptability
However alien and horrible others may seem to us at first, they are fellow human beings, seeking happiness for themselves and those close to them. Problems between people commence when one group seems to threaten the happiness of another. One side seeming to ignore or not understand the reason for the other's negative reaction reinforces the feeling of being threatened, leading to mutual negativity. 'Why on Earth can't they understand and change their ways!' one can hear both sides shouting unheard in so many world conflicts. So, matters worsen; until the negativity coming from both sides seems so outrageous that it is beyond forgiveness. Ultimately, one group can decide that whole cultures 'need to be destroyed'. With Hitler, it was Jewry. For Isil it seems to be all who deny the 'Caliphate'; including many Muslims.

In every age, place and culture, there is a firebrand Hitler ready to preach 'the final solution' to anyone willing to listen. Usually, he or she is an embarrassing eccentric grumbler, largely ignored on the fringes of society, even the corner of a bar or café. Why some people *are* listened to at particular times and places, needs to be asked and answered. We seek not to excuse, but to explain, how people, seeking happiness like us, came to think this way. In Germany between the wars, the suggestion that international Jewry was involved in the settlement after World War One was used to justify the persecution of all Jews throughout Europe. Pol Pot's literalist misunderstanding of Marxism led to the ethnic cleansing of Cambodia's middle classes.

Now it is Isil. We may just be able to grasp how its lethal extremism grew in Iraq and Syria, if we imagine the experience of living in Iraq since the 2003 invasion. In October 2013, the BBC reported a survey that estimated 461,000 died up to 2011. Imagine the 7-7, Paris or Brussels attacks being an everyday experience and 9-11 just one air attack of many, and all this seeming to be triggered by invading strangers. Might you feel that those strangers, those unbelievers and the people who sent them need to experience it too?

Forgiving the unacceptable
Of course, nothing justifies arbitrary killing. Also, when things reach extreme, uncompromising intolerance, security and physical protection are essential; even though we know that this may exacerbate the problem. Although the Treaty of Versailles created the environment that fostered Nazi Germany, Hitler still had to be defeated. However, the justification for the brutal war we waged was not only that we accepted serious past errors, but also were determined to create a better world after hostilities ceased.

Realising this, when the victors had defeated the unspeakable actions of Adolf Hitler, they did not repeat the errors of the post-World War One Versailles Peace Treaty. The post-World War Two agreement healed resentment and led to positive reform in the losing nations: Germany, Japan and Italy. The ringleaders were dealt with severely for their war crimes, but otherwise the slate was wiped clean. After that horrific death and sadness, all sides could breathe and rebuild together.

The consequences of the western powers' other disastrous decision after World War One remain to be addressed. Middle East policy at San Remo in 1920 and since has awakened and worsened the ancient tragedy of the area and opened a door for fanatics to drive through that agenda. As with Hitler, these fanatics must be defeated. As we do, the power of Isil, or a successor, to persuade and drive the agenda will weaken, but only to the greater or lesser extent that we admit to and correct our past mistakes.

Consider the scores of treaties the West has broken, resolutions ignored or blocked unreasonably; giving our 'friends' unfair political, military or commercial advantage. Have we plundered, wasted and lied? Every such decision, distortion and denial of rights has caused our present suffering. Being powerful, we assumed we had 'got away with it', maybe pushed our advantage even further. In fact, we have built massive resentment in those we made suffer. This has become a root rallying call; throwing so many potential friends into the arms of the fanatics that are always there, waiting to encourage our destruction.

Forgiveness in the twenty-first century
In the early decades of the twenty-first century, we need to do even more than move on and find forgiveness for the injustices that led to those 80 million World War Two deaths and today's Middle East hiatus. We need to address myriad negative feelings between billions of people throughout the world that have grown (mostly recognised only by the victims) for hundreds if not thousands of years. Immensely more than in Ireland after 'The Troubles', or in 1989 South Africa after apartheid, and, yes, more than in 1945 after World War Two. There is so much guilt and resentment, immense injustice and justifiable grounds for redress on all sides. A gross shadow of foreboding, the revenge of so many people hangs threateningly over us. No one feels secure.

In the face of this, it is pointless to struggle to defend, survive and seek to dominate. Millennia-long abandonment of principles causes attitudes that drive uncertainty and fear. These are made worse by relying on the rules, regulations, resolutions and policy actions that futile minds put into place, thinking they would protect them. Rules are no more than attempts to force the unwanted on the unwilling. By hiding behind them without agreement, and enforcing them brutally, unevenly and unjustly, we have caused our problems and continually make them worse.

All sides in all disputes have done just this. So, no amount of discussion about who did what when, should do now, and when to talk about it, will achieve anything. It will only make matters worse. When you fight for the truth, you cease to understand it. As after World War Two, we must wipe the slate clean, start afresh. Start by entering genuinely principled discussions that include everyone without pre-conditions. The survivors of a plane crash in isolated mountains have little use for anything beyond what keeps everyone alive, well and ready to contact helpers as soon as possible. Who was to blame or will be punished for the crash is of no use. Individual privilege and self-interest is sadly counterproductive.

So, in the world today, we must look for what will most effectively create not the world *one of us* thinks is best for everyone, but all kinds of harm-free worlds that *everyone can agree on*. To see clearly how to do this, first we need a major process of forgiveness. Whatever the past wrong, there must be a way to bring back together everyone as our family and friends.

Principles can unify motivation to a common purpose. Enlightened principles are the solution to all our problems.

.

Chapter 11
Open Borders - the Heart of the Answer

In the second half of the 1970s, as the world struggled to recover from the chaos of Vietnam and the Yom Kippur War with its consequent oil crisis, my wife and I went on a two-year pilgrimage, travelling overland from England to New Zealand.

This journey of awakening included: being with Greeks and Soviet Russians on a ship from the Black Sea, via Piraeus to Alexandria; travelling the Sahara Desert by Land Rover with an American, Canadian and Australian; enjoying the support of Egyptians; the remarkable hospitality of the Sudanese in the towns and villages of their vast country; the generosity of Jordanians in Aqaba and Irbid, as well as Israelis by the Sea of Galilee; the playfulness of Palestinians on an amazing south to north car ride through Syria; Iranian hospitality in Rasht and Mashhad; the primitive safety of the northern route of Afghanistan before the Russian invasion; travelling by train luggage rack in Pakistan; a wise and kindly welcome to India; Sikh generosity in Amritsar; the breathtakingly magical wisdom of Macleod Ganj; travelling to learn through adversity in India and Nepal; the two worlds of road and water that is Thailand; the rich fertility of Malaysia; being close to death in the jungles and rugged roads of Sumatra; the open-heartedness of Australia; to arrive in an 'antipodean Britain' of the 1950s that was New Zealand's Pakeha culture in 1979.

This life-awakening experience was fuelled by a lesson taught us at the Great Pyramid, near where we camped for over two weeks early in the journey. If we fear losing security, we will constantly experience insecurity. By accepting and working with insecurity we know where we are and hence feel secure. Armed with the confidence this gave us, the journey was made possible by a natural spirit of welcome and kindness from and to strangers in every culture and religious environment we visited.

The further one was from the cut and thrust of western and other outside cultures, in places little tainted by alien ways, the more this was so. At nearly every stage of the journey we felt blessed to be there to witness this, just before it was taken over by monocultural materialism. Its domineering self-righteousness always seemed to be close behind us, like a cancer creeping across the planet, seeping invasively to corrupt the kind open innocence of its healthy sub-culture cells.

We were ahead of it: on a virgin Cretan beach the year before a tourist hotel would be built to overlook it; camped out on the veranda of a deserted villa, not 200 yards across the sand from the Great Pyramid, before Giza became built up with urban sprawl; climbing to the Pyramid's very top, to hide and stay all night; to travel the troubled border between North and South Sudan; to get a bus from Jerusalem to Bethlehem, before the iron fence was erected; to stroll through deserted West Bank villages; sit in a lottery office in Aleppo, in times of peace; wander the poor areas of Egypt's Aswan and Afghanistan's Kabul, without fear of being kidnapped; hitchhike through Iran, Israel and Jordan; to be welcomed in remote Sumatran villages, play in the river with the children and be watched by the whole village as we ate dinner that night.

Imagine engaging in any of these activities in the twenty-first century, after four decades of invasion by force of arms or seductive consumerism, by those who care little for the culture they break in upon. In the intervening years, brutality has reached so much further into others' lives. At best, it has soured trust and friendship. At worst, events have created 'enemies' who wish for no more than to brutalise and ethnically cleanse us from the face of the Earth. Technology intrudes into people's homes. Opponents are attacked by drones, controlled from behind highly protected borders in distant lands. So many borders, more and more borders that trap us in ever smaller exclusive areas and ways of behaving for 'our own protection'!

Borders that do not protect

Nearly all the problems within and between groups in our world today are border issues created by fear and ignorance. Unnatural barriers enforced by physical security fences, police and armed forces are the product of mentally-assumed border issues between social groups and sub-cultures. We feel the need to protect wealth and possessions, our religion, countries, ideology, people and environment. There is a desperate need to know and hold on to what is mine and what is yours. There are walls between trade areas and, even within them, attempts to control immigration to sustain the advantages of indigenous populations. Then there are security walls to keep the poor from the private estates of the rich, and dress codes to ensure only the 'right sort of people' are present in places where the power games are played.

We are so caught up with the absolute need for borders, so intrinsically insecure, that we assume any discussion about the removal of borders should involve alternative protection in the form of a new set of conditions (i.e. a new set of borders!). We do not remove borders, merely move them. This is brutally and cynically so in many trade agreements, where double standards are taken to amazing heights of hypocrisy. Multinational companies and financial traders seek the freedom to trade, transfer currencies and speculate unhindered throughout the globe. At the same time, they insist on having long-standing intellectual property controls and restrictions on any actions of governments and local communities that might hamper their business activities. Their wish is a borderless world for the 'haves', protected by borders to keep out as many 'have nots' as possible; except, of course, as paying consumers!

The real removal of barriers between people involves accepting and allowing differences without question; having the personal courage and kindness to let down defences and open our hearts to each other. Compare Germany before and after the destruction of the Berlin Wall, South Africa before and after apartheid, the Southern States of the US, before and after segregation, the iron fence between Palestine and Israel. Places where barriers exist are the most miserable and insecure places on Earth, where even the most privileged and protected live continually on the precipitous edge of fear.

Then consider couples in a close relationship and generations in a family where feelings are so negative that old friends become strangers. Do not the barriers of negative projection, exclusion and unfriendly gossip we put up make us feel less secure, uncared for, more isolated?

Removing artificial borders; *Golden Standard* **second step**
However much we build walls, regulate, check and seek to control and contain what we perceive as being against our interests, whatever international, national or personal form they take, in the end only karma (the consequences of our previous actions) will control our borders!! However tightly we lock a dam's sluice gates, as water pressure increases, it will build and burst through somehow, some time. The wise engineer maintains an informed relationship with the water through respect for and understanding of its nature and needs, letting that inform his working of the gates. This way he establishes a natural flow for all concerned. Keeping out all water exposes us to ignorance of the ways of water and so the greatest danger of a disastrous collapse or overflow of the dam. So it is with African, Afghanistan, Muslim, Mexican, Palestinian, and all other refugees. World War Two resistance movements found a way to undermine rigid Nazi occupations, despite its policy of arbitrary mass reprisal. There are always ways to sneak in a wrongdoer and

undermine an enemy from inside. For these reasons, we should ensure we see the emergency defensive measures we take as being temporary.

Imagine a world without artificial borders, where people come and go as they will. See such a vision not as an immediate change, but a key ongoing aim: the second courageous step that will enable the principles of the *Golden Standard* to be what we live by. In this future world, people will not, as they do now, come to negotiations just to gain for themselves ('How little allowance for climate change can we get away with?' 'I'll tell them what they want to hear and then do what I like.'). The borderless principle turns this on its head. ('How much can we gain for everyone?' 'How can we contribute to the common good?') Thinking this way relaxes alienation between people, starts them working together in a new relief of reasonableness. A borderless world no longer seems dangerous and impossible.

When there is conflict in parts of the world, or economic imbalance between different areas, do we continue to profit by supplying arms to the warring factions, while we build our own defences, to keep escaping refugees from our land? Or would it be better to have international agreements to prevent arms sales (especially the bullets and shells for the weapons)? Should we invest in those parts of the world, so that no one wishes to make dangerous journeys to other lands? The movement of enormous waves of refugees and economic migration is a natural disaster created by corrupt international relations on all sides. A system of international conciliation, obligatory to all countries, should be established to reconcile warring parties, as they are starved of weapons. So much is possible when our overriding principle is that all should have life, liberty and happiness and the right to cross borders to find it; as it is between the states in the US.

Free movement in a borderless Europe was a vision the citizens of an expanding group of nations enjoyed for several decades. Now the fear of attack and politics of selfishness seek to put up protective barriers to sustain our own advantage, whatever the suffering of those outside. The joy of travelling as a friend, of being waved through so many different cultures, should not be a sub-group privilege for the few, to be defended against the rest from behind protective fences. It should be an ideal to be extended as soon as possible to the whole world; even if it does mean radical adjustments and difficult realities for those who have exploited and gained advantage by brutal force of arms.

To those entrenched in privilege living relatively safe, comfortable lives, such a possibility may seem unrealistic, the choices too hard to accept. Yet, make no mistake, until we are genuinely working toward it, there will be no real peace or happiness in the world, or in our personal lives.

Imagine instead the power for good of an increasing number of peoples acting on the commitment to make free movement and economic stability the key absolute aim for everyone. Consider facing up to the implications that such free movement would entail and putting real effort into making it a practical possibility.

Aim is the crucial word. Clearly the removal of all borders—be they political, economic, physical, mental or emotional—right away would lead to unimaginably chaotic consequences. As the Pluto-in-Capricorn period reaches its climax through to the early 2020s, most societies face insecurity and are turning in on themselves, desperately trying to hold on to the old ways. Many may see protectionism, nationalism, even racialism as the only way. Why people feel this way needs to be understood. Actions are needed to give positive reassurance by protecting the immediate future, without enshrining intolerance. In the UK, could taking back control through Brexit give the nation the confidence to open its doors to the world? All over the world, globalisation needs to include ways to redistribute its benefits to those who have lost most from its introduction.

Reassured in this way then, it will become clear that no border can be anything more than a first stopgap stage in the process to its removal. Look forward to the time when we can agree how it can be removed. Then work together to keep to or improve on that timetable. Above all, everyone involved must want to break down barriers that stand in the way. Then it will happen.

Celebrating and gaining from cultural differences
Paradoxically, the removal of artificial borders between peoples will empower and so enrich, not dilute, the world's wonderful cultural range. Some of us are tall, others short. People are skilled at myriad different activities. Some prefer the country, others the town, the theatre, the sports field, or to sit captivated before a computer screen. Christians celebrate Christmas, Diwali is the Hindu festival of lights, Jews call it Chanukah, Muslims observe Ramadan, Buddhists take purifying precepts every new and full moon. We like it like this. To feel free to celebrate these similar things in very different ways offers comfort to the participants and the joy of new experience and insights to any tolerant visitor.

Do we really want the same hotels, stores, fashion outlets, goods, and practices in every part of the globe? We struggle to protect the world's rich variety of animals and natural environments. Why not sustain and celebrate human diversity just as much? Why does twenty-first century humanity wish to standardise its many selves into one overwhelming constantly-striving hedonistic tedium? Paradoxically, it is today's so-called 'world free market economy' that creates many artificial barriers. Businesses profit by encouraging customers along narrow lines of consumption. Denying respect for differences empties our truly creative juices, leaves us enslaved in aspirations, defending a way of life few of us will ever attain, or would want if we did.

An ideal world is one of rich cultural variety, whose diverse ways are the collective expression of the people in that community or country. Cultures should be open to all visitors ready to observe the etiquette of the guest. How many problems in the Middle East emanate from westerners' failure in this regard?

There must be respect for differences. Trusting newcomers does not have to be detrimental. It may improve, not upset, the status quo. Changes that newcomers do make may well bring solutions. Their assimilation can be variously structured. Some will maintain their traditional heritages and live tolerantly alongside each other. Others will be integrated and generate a magnificent new hybrid. These, and varieties in between, will enrich the possibility and strength of the land they share. With this will come understanding between cultures throughout the world. With this will come a broader sense of family recognition. With such family feelings will come the wish that none should be exploited or go without. The natural human way of kindness will shine through to eradicate greed and provide resources for more and more throughout the world.

Doing better by having less
Such a view will mean considerable readiness to accept change. It will involve adjustments that seem to deprive us of what we are told we need. For better-off parts of the world, there could well be a transition to less money and fewer goods. Everyone may have to adjust to consuming less energy. How many lights do we need in order to see our way? How many varieties of food to build our bodies? How many types of car and how often need they be new? How much does each need to own exclusively, when we could share or help each other repair, not throw away? Is growth the only way to happiness? If we consume and work less, but share more, we will both receive and need less money. We will welcome this and be pleased to see we

remain free to live life as we wish. So, enjoying many new experiences of sharing with and giving to the community, as it seems right.

The crucial thing is not to think of where it will lead, the 'endgame'. How could we know, before we are there; if ever we are? Nor should we spend too long worrying about what is being sacrificed on the way. Focus instead on the principles that will make us feel better all the time. Does what we do today match the principled behaviour, upon which we wish our lives to be founded? If we can answer yes, we are on the right path. If no, then we have already diverted from a goal we are in danger of missing.

This new way of change must be vitally different from past revolutions, which went wrong by compromising their principles. By using their power early on to force sacrifice for an assumed long-term common good, the leaders merely dominated in a different, but rarely better, way. Failing to open the people's hearts with principles that create ongoing experience of endless possibility, they became little different to those that went before. In post-revolutionary France, Russia and many nations in more recent times, some of the new leaders are worse. We will not go that way, but rather take steady reasonable principled steps, letting our integrity open understanding, as we tread ever further away from our current system and its direction towards inevitable disaster.

At last an inheritance to be thankful for
It is a historical truism that children curse their parents and forebears for the tainted social conditions they leave for their descendants to resolve. How was Joseph so naive as to trap his people as virtual slaves in Egypt, or Moses to die before leading his people to the Promised Land? The crass decadence at the end of the Egyptian and Roman Empire exposed their descendants to destruction and conquest. The Roman Church's degeneracy and the self-righteousness of

many Christian sub-groups led the world to centuries-long religious conflict.

Our times can be different. Globalisation, where more countries and multinational corporations act to create a neo-colonial world economy, may not be sustainable. Yet, paradoxically, it is the dangerous ever-expanding power of our times to consume and destroy that forces us to transform this false start into an enlightened form of globalisation. Now could be a key time for good in world history, when we stop making things worse, turn circumstances around and leave an improved heritage for our descendants. There are three main reasons for such optimism.

- Firstly, the power and knowledge we have to destroy could well be used to repair, restore and care for each other and the planet.
- Secondly, for the first time in recorded history humanity has the capacity to know and communicate throughout the Earth, to understand from many perspectives. Not only leader to leader, but the people can talk directly to each other.
- Thirdly, astro-cycles in the early twenty-first century indicate a rare threshold that challenges us to turn away from potential disaster and embark upon positive change. However impossible events may be coming to be, coming also will be an option to continue with an important liberation of human consciousness. The cyclic stages of this growth can be traced astrologically from the sixteenth through the eighteenth centuries to our time.

We have seen that this urge for independent co-creation with each other is the way of genuine hard-headed economic reality; the essential unbelievably radical change needed in the way we do business with each other. Despite the scientific over-optimism that human ingenuity will find a way around it, we will be confronted with the limitations of the planet. Astro-cycles suggest we could be approaching a time as significant as the third millennium BCE Bronze Age.

Astro-cycles and global disintegration

Chapter Two started us on this quest for a better world, by citing the ongoing triple conjunction of Jupiter, Saturn and Pluto in Capricorn as an indication of the world facing unavoidable economic and social reality toward the end of the 2010s. This could be dire, but does not have to be if we embrace change with the right motivation.

Completing this four-year writing project in 2016, there are many reasons to fear the worse for the future. The year's Saturn in Sagittarius and Neptune in Pisces square period has brought misinformation, laced with hatred, into our dealings with each other. The paths of negativity that many groups, nations and their leaders seem embarked upon could indeed be stepping stones to the Mad Max dystopian world, visualised in the Miller-Kennedy films. It will happen if we are unwilling to let go of narrow selfish interests. When there is no compromise, there can only be a clash of Titans; everyone loses, only destruction reigns. The courageous will stand up tall with better answers to avert such a disaster.

Astro-cycles and global regeneration

If social and economic change based on cooperation to help everyone do and receive the very best becomes the ideal, we will pass through fear and uncertainty to increasingly enlightened and easier life experiences. Astro-cycles set the stage, leaving humanity, and other sentient beings, to act on it as they wish. Because the stage is limited, there are karmic consequences. So constantly we need to consider where we are and what we want.

On the Winter Solstice, 21st December 2020, Jupiter and Saturn come together in the first degree of Aquarius. In the coming year(s), they will mark a path for Pluto's transit there

2023-43. If Pluto in Capricorn 2008-24 has focused us on the regeneration of the world's political and economic structure, the Pluto in Aquarius period will focus us upon the regeneration of our attitude towards the way knowledge serves humanity and the life and fabric of the planet.

The transit and then mutual reception of Uranus and Neptune in Aquarius and Pisces 1995-2011, along with Pluto in Sagittarius through that time, saw the unbalanced obsession with materialistic, reductionist science, discussed in Chapters Four and Nine. If not contained by the *Golden Standard* principles, the 2020s will, at best, see increasingly artificial, impersonal societies, where powerless individuals depend on experts to rule their lives. At worst, destructive social breakdown will indeed bring in a Mad Max world.

There is no need for such pessimism. We have access to information and can question experts and authority systems more than ever before. Most scientists are good people, seeking knowledge for the benefit of humanity. Their concern to combat climate change is a clear indication of this. Developing from here into a broader, ethically-based nature-focused research into new areas could revolutionise our lives for the better. We must do more, yet use less energy and find renewable ways of creating it. We need methods to maintain such sources, pollution-free for centuries, even millennia.

The ideal expression of Pluto in Aquarius is science involving and integrating all knowledge: quantitative and qualitative, ancient and modern, genetics and astrology, naturopathic and allopathic medicine.

The 'water' that the symbol of Aquarius pours down from its vase is, in fact, the wise air of understanding that liberates humanity from ignorance. In short, when all wisdom is allowed in, it enables the very *Golden Standard* of principles that is the positive core of this book. Let us read about them again and start to make them so in our lives!
By learning from and then rising above the Capricorn realism of the 2010s, wise, caring people may well begin to

recognise a glimmer of the first light of hope in the Aquarian Jupiter-Saturn conjunction at that 2020 Winter Solstice.

In his *Planetary Cycles Mundane Astrology*, the great French astrologer, André Barbault, demonstrates the incredible accuracy of his planetary Cyclic Index in projecting major twentieth-century global conflict, tension, even war.[51] The index for the years 2010-25 show the most extreme negative, and then positive, indications of the whole of the 1900-2100 period. With kindness and *Golden Standard* principles, we can use this to dissolve nastiness and keep on creating a better world for us all.

Reversing the race to global destruction

Civilisation is the product of many cycles, but experience ensures that we never return untouched to where we were before. If we are foolish, we fall below, to learn and struggle our way upward again. If we are wise, we rise above like a spiral, seeing new, improved uses for wisdom, marshalling past knowledge with more enlightened eyes.

As we move through to the 2020s, there comes a challenge to break a disingenuous pattern. To end those greed-based lies of narrow self-interest that have raped and pillaged civilisations and the planet for 5,000 years. To give it fresh air, when it is just at the point where it gasps helplessly for breath. By offering our children the way to work toward a multicultural world without artificial borders, sustained by principles that guide every action we take, we will be one of the first generations in history to offer hope to future generations.

The planetary liner's rush to the iceberg of disaster will be slowed, halted and turned, as the race to global destruction starts to be reversed.

Chapter 12 - Let's Get Real!

It may seem that during the four years to 2016 it has taken to write this book, world events have hijacked and fundamentally undermined the ongoing idealism of its message. 'Let's get real! How can we leave our borders open, let alone relax them even further, to so many people, who may include some who behead charity workers? How can we reach an understanding with suicide bombers, motivated by a vision of heaven, whose entry ticket is the mass destruction of "infidels"? How can we see hope in ordinary people, when masses of them seem more ready to hit out and accuse, than understand and care for strangers in need?'

Looking astrologically, the cycles for the years immediately before us suggest we stand at the threshold of a very different new world. This may well be for worse, but we can still make it for the better. We should not be discouraged. Disintegrating change, however radical, can be stressful, but such astro-events do not mean bad things will happen. Inevitable evil is never written in the stars; incredible difficulties often are. The best outcomes arise when we take on difficulties and transform them into benefits.

Setbacks should encourage us to go forward
Part One of this book revealed how and why we find ourselves in today's difficult situations. *Part Two* looked deeper and suggested a mindset to put them right. When the worst of all things happens, only a vision of unity can bring goodness. Imagine everyone coming together to enjoy in their own way those unique things they love in a world that tolerates innumerable differences. Chapter 10 reminded us that such a vision after World War Two enabled Germany and Japan to become havens of peace and efficiency. Having cut out intolerant evil, the post-World-War-One errors were

replaced with kind, generous forgiveness, even respect, by the victors. This created the gratitude of peace that we still enjoy with those nations to this day. It enabled an open Europe and wider world of exchange and cooperation.

Handling setbacks that undermine ordinary life
In less immediately dangerous times, the issues of this book may easily have passed by most people living their day-to-day lives. They may have felt: 'It is all so serious! Why bother; what is all the fuss about?' For in many, even perhaps most, cultures, both rich and poor, people experience much pleasure in lives full of fun, friends, comfort and close family ties. They enjoy eating drinking, dancing, singing and celebrating, sport, leisure and celebrity gossip, making love, and engaging in zany adventures; worrying about their appearance and fashion and what friends think about them. Life is precious and most people see such everyday pleasure in the experience of it as the very centre of everything.

The great issues of the world may be important, but for most of the time politicians and intellectual processes that stand up to address these great issues seem hardly worth knowing about. A vast chasm of impossibility seems to exist between people's day-to-day experiences, responsibilities and pleasures and their capacity for effective action on the big issues. So they soldier on, avoiding what they do not like about the system and demanding as much as they can gain from it.

Then attacks like 9-11, London 2005, 2015-16 Paris and Brussels and racially-motivated killings in the US savagely intrude and demand the attention of the populace at large. Ordinary people have their work and play cut through and apart by bombs and bullets. Newscasts repeatedly show the aftermath; so, millions experience what could well have happened to them as well. Worldwide outrage and generous expressions of sympathy soon turn to retaliation, restrictions on freedom, more spending on protection. Then come calls to arms, which turn sour as combatants die horribly. Only war profiteers celebrate. So it is or has been in Syria, Iraq, Vietnam, London, Berlin, Dresden, Hiroshima, Flanderss Fields and beyond; and where else by the time you read this book?

Good heals wounds
Only those reared in psychotic societies and sub-groups seek to blame, terrorise and possess others. None of these represent the fundamental way of the world. Beneath any horror, aching to be heard, are nearly everyone's natural feelings of wanting to be kind and principled, as described in Chapter 8. Deep kindness grounding the heart of human nature can be found in every major world religion and humane philosophy. It is there when we cut through the barriers of institutionalised attachment that insist 'my way is the only way'.

The heart of Christianity is focused on redemption that comes from putting one's own needs after those of others; the capacity to forgive, to love our enemies, whatever the wrongdoing. Islam is rooted in submission to divine oneness; the safeness, truth and peace that comes from leading a virtuous life of prayer, personal restraint and generosity to others. Judaism virtuously maintains and experiences the consequences of a special relationship with an all-seeing unfathomable divine mind. Knowing that karmic consequences are inevitable, Buddhists let go of illusory attachments of the body, speech and mind, focus on that true nature of Sunyata and generate compassion. Once we realise that Hindu and Ancient Greek gods are devices of psychological cleansing, we see their beliefs are focused upon a similar centre of oneness: known as Brahma to the Hindus, or the creative power of love generating life out of an abyss of chaos to the Ancient Greeks. Shamanistic, pagan and naturalistic cultures recognise, respect and develop an exemplary sustaining relationship with their natural world environment. Nearly all people welcome strangers who come with respect, not just to take and threaten. In one way or another, the world's spiritual practices teach there are unavoidable consequences for any wrongdoing. Kindness and cooperation has been the first and most profound refuge in human nature throughout its history. Carnivorous animals kill to eat, not with a lust to harm.

Yet always there has been a problem. We accept this intrinsic goodness in life and wish to tolerate, understand and sustain it, but how do we handle those ravaging hordes that come from over the hills to steal and ravish all we have? Nowadays, they are those with means of lethal physical or financial force that dominate, lie to, tempt and so corrupt vulnerable minds.

There are ways. For although armed force and controlling communication are far mightier in our time, we have the ability to move around and pass on information. This makes it much easier to know about, see what is coming and defeat corrupt power in advance.

Over the past 500 years, citizens have demanded they be more than vassals of an all-powerful nobility. The recognition of individual rights has grown. Within and even between many nations, we have seen more gentleness and humanity; fewer employ public punishment, or even wish to use physical violence against prisoners. The death penalty is used in fewer countries. There is wider tolerance of minorities. Citizens see through and stand up against temptation and intimidation more than ever before

We can create a better world. Look around! See the signs of it coming together! Alongside the social ravages of nineteenth-century industrialisation came great philanthropic institutions against slavery, and then child exploitation. Then came trades unions, universal education, achieving ever-wider voter franchises. Recent decades have seen massive expansion in the range of people participating in and contributing to charities. For many of us, it is unacceptable that people and animals should suffer sickness, go without food or shelter. Moved by such suffering, millions take pleasure in and contribute to telethons, stirred on by stories of human need. Tragedies in the news can activate immense public outpourings of grief.

Those who care most deeply go 'left-field' to the conventional view, seeking more radical ways to change the status quo. Action on global warming, ecological movements, yoga, meditation, mindfulness training are all becoming a part of day-to-day life, in work as well as leisure. In such ways, more and more of us seek a better quality of life for all. The response to the principles upon which President Obama was elected; more recently, the humane messages of His Holiness Pope Francis; the packed halls to hear His Holiness the Dalai Lama's message of humanity's common wish for universal happiness: all show that when people feel the way of the good heart is possible, they welcome its message. They gladly embark upon its path. There is a groundswell of kindness, an undercurrent wishing all well, the healing power of goodness urging to find expression in almost everyone.

It is not just a special minority of do-gooders; everyone seeks a better world. Witness the healing power of great music; the communal joy of audiences listening together; the life-changing catharsis when we identify with a tragic hero. By doing good, we heal all wounds. It *is* as simple as that.

Give goodness time to grow
The aim of this book has been to expose the practical incompetence of a world grounded upon *caveat emptor* let the buy beware, which leads to the institutionalisation of meanness and manipulation. By understanding this, we remove the obstacles that such limited self-centredness puts in the way of a happy, healthy planet.

Broader and deeper analysis brings us to mature, wiser decisions about what to do next. We see how better relations with each other could create a future that is empty of ignorance and brute negativity. Knowing self-confirming interconnected institutions run the planet, and so hold joint responsibility for our world problems, empowers our minds to see where change is needed!

When we do, we are immediately faced with another danger — the temptation to start believing in and fighting for an ideal alternative society. This error comes from expecting too much and then closing our minds to learning as we go. By rigidly visualising a purist 'utopian' end game, anyone not sharing this vision appears to be an enemy, needing to be put down for the greater good. The French Reign of Terror in the 1790s and Stalinist purges of the 1930s are two of many examples. Once in power, it is so easy to forget the bright vision that first motivated our quest. Difficulties and compromises faced on the way can manipulate our minds to focus uncritically on the interests of the new ruling group and its friends. Unwittingly we accept...'everyone wishes the ideal we all seek were attainable, but *in the real world*, we have to accept...' Soon we too are bereft of principle. Idealism fades back to the same old story.

The antidote to such a losing our way is to hold to the *Golden Standard* principles explained in Chapter 8, with all our being, uncompromisingly, every moment. Accept that nothing is certain, except that real improvement comes only when everything we feel, think and do is founded upon that unshakeable *Golden Standard* principle. Also, real change requires ongoing correction; including reconsideration and purification of the corrections already made. For real change comes when we are clear about principles and use them constantly to clarify and correct actions. This process takes time but, when approached like this, the reassuring joy of fully resolving issues increases exponentially. By being clear about what is happening and the motivation and clarity of those around us, we feel content and empowered to carry on. Such understanding and adherence to principle can sustain us through the worst of times; even when faced with privation created by the deluded or evil intentions of others. That we understand and have done the best we can leaves our minds clear, our energy intact to find ways to improve the direst circumstances.

Not an impossible dream
Many will still feel that the adoption of such idealism just won't happen. Utopia on Earth is impossible. It is not in our nature. It's an every-creature-for-itself Universe. Because we cannot do everything right away does not mean we cannot do anything at all. Only a fool restricts arguments for a better future to those that can be switched on immediately, like an electric light. The wise person knows that the best way to live is in a decent principled present all the time.

This world is a place of learning. There may never be heaven on Earth, but let the Earth be a place where all beings have a chance to move on the way to enlightened understanding. Utopia is not an endgame, but the experience of living a principled life that moves ever closer to achieving it. Because people continue to kill and steal, we do not give up and say there is nothing to be done about murder and robbery. Rather we continue to strive for a world without them.

By identifying and publicising ideal ways, we put up a touchstone, a guide, a measure, by which to judge the behaviour of anyone seeking authority over us. How close are their aims and actions to the ideal *Golden Standard*? Ensuring right answers will avoid many false options and their consequentially disastrous outcomes. Reject all calls to sacrifice principles in the service of expediency in 'the real world'. Such is the way to inefficiency, injustice and ongoing suffering. Pluto in Capricorn demands real sustainable, principle-based efficiency.

Principled people are not just unrealistic idealists; they are the practical realists. Let no one whose deeds do not stand up to the *Golden Standard* convince you they have values or policies likely to withstand the changing pace of time. The more we stand against compromise, the more lastingly successful and happier our world and our lives will be.

Not a dream at all
There will not be any real change if this adherence to principle is a dream that moves our emotions far more than it influences the actions we take. We should start with ourselves: be mindfully attentive to our own thoughts and actions. See the good, the very best, in others and make this a positive part of ourselves. Then we will be on the road that enables the freedom of genuine victory for all.

The Anthem of Love

Prologue

Stand back!
Stand back from the pain and pressure
Of what is always assumed to be true.

Look deep!
Look deeper than has ever been seen
Into the heart of unifying truth.

Look wide!
Look wider than human gaze has ever dared
Into ultimate reaches of understanding that make us one.

Be beyond resentments at what 'they have done',
Beyond the burning desire to have 'what we do not have',
Beyond blame, fear, revenge, and prejudice,
Beyond the obsession with 'defence',
Beyond that personal uncertainty that hardens
And isolates us from the ecstasy

Of opening into love for all.

Let all assumptions melt away!
What has been wrong can cease right now
And was not meant that way at all.
All who suffer create the cause of their own suffering.
We hate in others what we see as hateful in ourselves.

Armaments are the way of frightened people,
Trembling lest past misdemeanours return to haunt them.
Violence the action of cornered men,
Outraged and desperate at being starved of love.
No law or treaty has, can, or will protect us.

No one is to blame: all share the responsibility for
The love we lost, the close one who died,
The fortune we missed, the disgrace we endure,
The lack of response, the failure to understand,
Colonial and world wars, starvation, pollution,
Corruption, the nuclear danger, genocide,
Racial persecution, concentration camps,
Palestine, Indo-China, Tiananmen Square,
Ethiopia, South America, drug-running,
Laws that deny the right of personal choice,
Defensive medicine, cartels, barriers,
Bureaucracy, defenders of the indefensible,
The unfeeling pomposity of many parliaments and politicians,
Calculated statements made for effect to hide the truth,
Materialistic science interested only in perpetuating itself,
Without regard for people on the planet,
Funding and investment for short-term selfish gain;
All have their causes and their cures with ourselves!
So, seek not to divide and argue over the responsibility.
Look not outside, but within yourself for blame.

The test of wisdom is to grasp the moment!
The test of wisdom is to change right now!

The Anthem of Love

Rise up in love to the constant glory of new opportunity!
Rise up in love to enrich and make a better world!
Rise up in love so each celebrates the part they play!
Rise up in love that is beyond needing, seeking or expectation!
Rise up in a love that is constantly grateful!

Listen to nature:
See how it adapts, accommodates,
And uses everything to make a place for all.
Let the success of our love be measured
In the richness of life in our oceans and rivers,
The greenness of our forests, the natural fertility of our soil,
The evenness of our climates, the joy of living.
Glorify a planet unified in diversity.

Listen to the Universe:
See its totality within and without ourselves,
See the fair balance of its justice.
Nothing happens that does not need to be,
Yet we are free to make existence even more.
No opportunity is ever lost, no problem eternally with us.
See continual balance as a benefit for all.
Rise to the immaculate. Know total control.

Celebrate the best in all that exists:
The struggle of the young child seeking to know,
The withdrawal of the old preparing to go.
All that is completes us;
A treasured rich cultural tapestry beyond compare.
The ingenuity of the technological mind,
The incisive insight of the devoted mystic,
The public servant's sense of duty,
The dissenter's courage and honour,
The love of the Jew and Palestinian
For their homeland - that earthly precious jewel,

The good intentions of law and justice,
The creative courage of all seekers of new experience,
The devotion and magical skill of the Hindu,
The religious integrity of the Muslim,
The dedication to sacrifice and service of the Christian,
The compassion and pure practice of the Buddhist,
The natural wisdom of the native,
The conscience of the socialist,
The courage of the capitalist,
The skill and efficiency of the German,
The enduring persistence of the British,
The youthful enthusiasm of the North American,
The way of celebration of the tropical races,
The patience of the Chinese,
The efficiency of the Japanese,
The dance of Africa,
The wisdom of Asia,
The muscle of Europe,
The beauty and variety of the Americas,
The ancient and new in Australasia,
The emptiness of the Arctic and Antarctic,
The rich variety of our oceans,
The openness of the air,
The fruits of the earth,
The infinite potential in our actions,
The balanced movement of our solar system,
Our place in our galaxy, the Universe.
All is one in love. In love, we see it so.

Pour out true love from open hearts!
Touch, dedicate, create, see unity in diversity,
Have room for all.
Let bright-eyed tears of celebration
Pour out amidst the ringing bells of joy!

Victory! Victory!
Victory - beyond revenge!

Victory - beyond thought of the next battle!
Victory - that is constantly renewed!
Victory - that relies on no one but ourselves!
Victory - that grows in constant climax!
Victory - that sees no evil!
Victory - where what is wrong just fades away!
The virgin touch of appropriate contact,
The completeness of an intercourse
That continually surprises, beyond any need to expect.

Love that opens us to the stars
In understanding of all that can ever be.
Love that is the constant continuation of itself.
Love that makes us eternally free.

Now that's what's real!

Notes

[1] https://en.oxforddictionaries.com/word-of-the-year/word-of-the-year-2016
[2] Roy Gillett Preface, *Economy Ecology and Kindness,* 2009.
[3] Ibid.
[4] Even worse are those who were not in power at the time, who try to pretend that in the same circumstances they would have behaved any differently to those who were.
[5] Roy Gillett, Preface, *Economy Ecology and Kindness,* 2009.
[6] Non-astrologers will find my *The Secret Language of Astrology* 2011 Duncan Baird Publishers a most useful introduction to learning the astro concepts and how to use them.
[7] Roy Gillett, *Economy Ecology and Kindness,* Pages 84-5.
[8] Ibid. Studies the astrology of the development of unsupported credit from the deregulation of the banks in US, UK and much of the rest of the world since the early 1980s. In 1991, Robert Maxwell disappeared in suspicious circumstances, having engaged in dubious accounting to sustain the value of his share portfolio. Looking back from today, his wish and methods to create illusions of value to sustain an already bankrupt enterprise are little more than a John-the-Baptist-type heralding of twenty-first century economics.
[9] At the time of writing, hundreds of thousands of people are crossing vast deserts and dangerous oceans for the chance of being grudgingly allowed to live in prosperous countries.
[10] The Bank of England was founded to raise funds to manage loans to the British government. Early resources were devoted to the re-building of the British Navy, which became the cornerstone of the expanding British Empire. It was this, and other European countries who followed its imperial example, that established the economic principles that have directly developed into today's world economic principles.
[11] For more details of this see Roy Gillett, *Economy Ecology and Kindness* Chapter 3, Page 27,
[12] Ibid
[13] Ibid
[14] Reported by Bloomberg in May 2015. http://www.bloomberg.com/news/articles/2015-05-08/china-s-very-high-mountain-of-debt.
[15] https://www.theguardian.com/business/2016/jun/16/chinas-debt-is-250-of-gdp-and-could-be-fatal-says-government-expert.
[16] BBC Teletext 26th September 2016.
[17] Does not end completely until Pluto leaves Capricorn 2023-4.

[18] Because the astrological chart is a complex matrix of negative-positive, yin-yang, expressive-receptive, archetypal male-female qualities, it acknowledges and allows for and respects every shade of sexual orientation. Quite simply, astrology makes us capable of respecting everyone for what they are.

[19] A Buddhist expression quoted by HH The Dalai Lama in *Toward a True Kinship of Faiths* 2010 Doubleday Religion

[20] Terence McKenna *Food of the Gods* 1992 Bantam Books. This looks over thousands of years from humanity's first time on earth to show the relationship between various substances and cultural assumptions.

[21] There are eight bars selling alcohol in the British Houses of Parliament. Hence the legality of other drugs is decided by people under the influence of alcohol; hardly culturally objective! Maybe close bars and no alcohol consumed by members for two months before such legislation is considered?

[22] Allowing for the 33% who did not vote, the 2015- UK Conservative Government is supported by less than 25% of the electorate and the Labour opposition by just under 20%

[23] In fact the RAND Corporation mathematically studied strategies on how to succeed in cheat-based Games Theory, aptly known as 'Fuck you buddy'. Is this the only possible society? See Roy Gillett, *Astrology and Compassion the Convenient Truth* Pages 166-7.

[24] Chapter 4 shows that today's mechanical way of understanding and determining actions based on reductionist science, is as much a belief system as any of the traditional religions.

[25] Roy Gillett, *The Secret Language of Astrology* 2012 Duncan Baird Ltd.

[26] A more fruitful way of understanding time may be to stop viewing it as linear; rather to see the past, present and future as eternal and interdependent. In this way behaviour in the present and future can be seen as the cause of past experiences. By seeing things that way, at least we can lay the past to rest by good selfless, generous actions in the present. Retribution in the present only stirs and exacerbates what happened; it keeps the horror of its memory living constantly in our tormented minds.

[27] http://englishhistoryauthors.blogspot.co.uk/2014/01/the-royal-medicine-monarchs-longtime.html AND
http://www.telegraph.co.uk/news/health/news/11739270/Queens-physician-calls-for-more-homeopathy-on-NHS.html

[28] Who knows what else by the time you read this book.

[29] The potential benefits of using astrology in education are considered in detail in Chapter 9.

[30] 'Chakravarti is an ancient Indian term used to refer to an ideal universal ruler,[1] who rules ethically and benevolently over the entire world. Such a ruler's reign is called sarvabhauma. It is a bahuvrīhi, figuratively meaning "whose wheels are moving", in the sense of "whose chariot is rolling everywhere without obstruction"'. [http://en.wikipedia.org/wiki/Chakravartin]

[31] *Rights of Man* by Thomas Paine leading to the American and French revolutions

[32] This word is coined for this book to invite comparison between the similar advantages and foibles, and possibly the destinies of the Edwardian aristocracy and 21st century middle classes.

[33] Fund raisings by Comic and Sports Relief television extravaganzas, or major city fancy dress marathons come to mind.

[34] Vance Packard, *The Hidden Persuaders* 1958 exposed the methods that have recently been brilliantly dramatised in the Lionsgate Television series *Mad Men*.

[35] *Invictus* a film, produced and directed by Clint Eastwood, depicting Nelson Mandela's role in South Africa's victory in the 1995 Rugby World Cup.

[36] There are institutions that consider ethical factors behind research methods and can act to contain implementation of discoveries. Also, most countries licence the use of new medicines. These restraints are extrinsic to the actual practice of reductionist science. They are administered by institutions whose ethical foundations, while maybe well intended, have no clearly grounded criteria of self-assessment.

[37] 'Her day is typical of that of most South Korean teenagers. She rises at 6.30am, is at school by *8am*, finishes at *4pm* (or *5pm* if she has a club), then pops back home to eat. She then takes a bus to her second school shift of the day, at a private crammer or hagwon, where she has lessons from *6pm until 9pm*.'   www.bbc.com/news/education-25187993.

[38] Tao Te Ching (602-531BC).

[39] It is not without some irony that Shakespeare gives this profound insight to the unfortunate Polonius, when advising his son Laertes, who was about to depart for England. In the event, misunderstanding and the dark deeds of others shortens both their lives. This does not undermine the value of the words. William Shakespeare *Hamlet*.

[40] For the complete *Rules of Acquisition*, based on *caveat emptor* let the buyer beware, the legal basis of today's commerce, see: http://projectsanctuary.com/

[41] *The Essential Chögyam Trungpa* Edited by Rose Gimian, 1999 Shambhala

[42] These ideas are developed more extensively in *Growing Pains* Alex Trenoweth, 2013 My Spirit Books.

43 1822 UT 21st December 2020.
44 'The government of the people, by the people, for the people, shall not perish from the Earth.' were the actual words of Abraham Lincoln's Gettysburg Address
45 For a fuller in-depth study, obtain the web talk 'Y851 The Middle East: Past, Present and Future' by R Hakan Kirkoglu with Roy Gillett at http://www.astrologicalassociation.com/shop/recordings/conference2013_recordings.html
46 Negotiations regarding way to break up the Ottoman Empire started as early as 1915. The key reshaping of the Middle East was established at this April 1920 San Remo Conference, except for Turkey . This took a rebellion and renegotiation until 1924 to complete.
47 André Barbault *The Value of Astrology* 2014 The Astrological Association, Chapter 7.
48 The nature of the men's actions is shown by their planets' links with the Jupiter-Neptune axis in the 1920 and 2002 charts George W Bush 0726 EDT, 6th July 1946, New Haven CT; Tony Blair 0610 BST, 6th May 1953, Edinburgh, UK.
49 'How the Islamic State evolved in an American prison' by Terrence McCoy, *The Washington Post*, November 4th 2014
50 English and French diplomats, whose 1916 outline arrangements for the reconstruction of the Middle East were generally adopted at the San Remo and associated conferences.
51 Especially see the diagrams on pages 150-51 of Chapter 14, *Planetary Cycles Mundane Astrology* 2016, The Astrological Association.

Index

A Passage to India 58
Academia 26
Academic 9, 71, 99, 127
Afghanistan 166, 167, 169
Africa(n) 40, 98, 100, 102, 189,
   North Africa 157
   South Africa 51, 164, 169, 193
Alawite Shia people 148
Alexander the Great 110
Allopathic 57, 58, 60, 127, 177
America(n/s) 46, 69, 82, 153, 166, 189, 193-194
   North America 189
   South America(ns) 40, 98, 100, 187
Anarch(y/ist) 46, 124
Anthem of Love, The 186-190
Apartheid 51, 164, 169
Arab 46
Aristocr(acy/atisation) 40, 69, 77, 78-79, 82-86, 193
Arms 11, 16, 98-99, 144, 161, 167, 170
Antarctic 189
Artic 189
Astrological Quartet 10, 138
Astrology and Compassion: the Convenient Truth 142-143, 192
Atheists 71
Autism 58
Ba'ath Party 153
Babylon 77, 110
Baghdad 111
Bank of England 22, 28-30, 32, 191
Bankers 13, 69, 94, 144
Barbault, André 150, 178, 194
Beckham, David 80
Berlin 181
Berlin Wall 82, 169
Biological 52

Black holes 52
Black Tuesday 23
Blair, Tony 152, 194
Blind Men and the Elephant, The 94
Brave New World 60, 63, 80
Bristol 98
Britain 91, 94, 111, 115, 147-148, 166
British Navy 29, 191
Bronze Age 176
Buddha
   Dharma 10
   Gautama 118, 121
Buddhist(s) 51, 120, 172, 181, 189, 192
   Bodhicitta 51
Burka 155, 158
Burkini 155
Bush, George W. 83, 151, 152 154
Cambodia 162
Canada 40
Capitalism 14, 26, 28, 30, 33, 34, 82, 89, 111, 132
Capitalist 14, 83, 84 189
   class system 84
   system 15, 17, 23, 25, 84, 99, 100, 102, 104, 106, 114
Casino 33
Century
   seventh 157
   thirteenth 111
   fifteenth 68, 77, 111-112
   sixteenth 17, 69, 77, 98, 111, 175
   eighteenth 17, 40, 69-70, 78, 175
   nineteenth 51, 70, 72, 78, 83-84, 182
   twentieth 10, 56, 78, 98, 111-112, 118
   twenty-first 35, 40, 50, 56, 72, 111, 121, 157-158, 164, 167, 172, 175, 191, 193
Chanukah 172
Chekov, Anton 85

Chemical(s) 57, 60, 63-64
Cherry Orchard, The 85
China 34, 36-37, 77, 100, 103, 105, 187, 191
   Chinese 36, 37, 40, 98, 189
Christian(s/ity) 46, 68, 72, 111-13, 145, 157, 172, 175, 181, 189
Christmas 44, 95, 172
Civil litigants 125
Class 85
   capitalist 84
   merchant 77
   middle 36, 83, 162, 193
   ruling 86
   social 64, 83
   under- 85
   working 83,
Cold War 82
Colonial(ism) 10, 33, 35, 40, 82, 98, 99, 102, 157, 175, 187
   exploitation 35
   neo- 10, 99, 175
   post- 35
   power(s) 33, 98-99
Complementary medicine 59
Confuci(us/an) 76, 116-118, 121, 128, 159
Consumer(ism) 47, 79, 91, 100, 167-168
   Consumption 12, 14, 27, 35-36, 38, 70, 85-86, 172
Corporation tax 11
Council of Nicaea 112
Creationist 66, 72
Credit Default Swaps 24, 36
Criminal
   process 47
   profit 47
   system 125
Crucifixion of Jesus Christ 144
Crusade(r/s) 157, 147, 153

Cycle - Jupiter and Saturn 20, 133, 176
Cyclic Index 178
Dalai Lama, His Holiness the 5, 183, 192
Dark Ages 68, 127
Dark matter 52
Darwin, Charles 66, 72
   Darwinists 72
Das Kapital 83
Debt(s) 12, 14, 35-38, 104, 115, 191
   exposure 37
Democracy 69, 70, 82, 96, 151
Divine Right of Kings 69
Diwali 172
DNA 61, 167
Dot-com 22-23
Dow Jones Industrial Price Index 21
Dresden 181
Drug laws 47-48
Duchess of Cambridge 80
Duke of Zhou 117
Earth 52, 70, 83, 122, 136, 142, 156, 162, 167, 169, 175, 185, 188, 189, 192, 194
Eastern religions 113
Economist(s) 11, 13, 35-7, 79, 114
Econom(y/ic) 9-17, 20, 23-25, 27-29, 31-42, 44, 51, 64, 73-74, 81-86, 93-95, 100-101, 106, 112-113, 115, 127, 131-135, 158, 170-171, 175-177, 191
   collapse 12, 36
   cycle 14, 37
   expansion 25
   system 11, 28, 40
Economy Ecology and Kindness 13-15, 24, 36, 191
Educational system(s) 74, 104
Egypt(ian/ians) 77, 110, 166-167, 174

Index

Eight Worldly Dharmas 120
Einstein 53
Electra 87
Electric(al) 52, 64, 99, 185
Emerging countries 34, 98
Empire(s) 77-78, 110
  British 191, 194
  Ottoman 111, 147, 194
  Persian 110
  Roman 112, 174
Employer(s) 14, 30, 81, 83-84
English and Welsh Civil Procedure Rules 47, 126
Enlightenment, the 62, 66, 70, 130
Esoteric 72
Ethical standards 31
Ethnic cleansing 16, 99, 162
Europe(an) 82, 85, 94, 99, 100, 103, 111-112, 156-157, 162, 170, 180, 189, 191
  medieval 77
European Central Bank 38
European Union 13, 94
Exploit(/ed/ers/ative) 13-16, 23, 25-26, 28, 30, 33-35, 40, 51. 64, 80, 82-84, 89, 91-94, 98-99, 102, 104-106, 114, 120, 135, 144, 156, 158, 171, 173, 182,
Exploitative capitalism 26, 33-34, 89
Faith school(s) 72
Fascism 82, 93, 103
Ferengi 118
Financ(ed/ial/ially) 9, 13-14, 24, 26, 30-31, 35-39, 41, 47, 71, 79, 92, 94, 101, 106, 115, 125, 127, 133-134, 144, 161, 168, 182,
  Regulation 26
Flanders Fields 181
Forster, E.M. 158
Fox News 88
Frack(ing) 81, 101
France 147, 153, 174

French 69, 147, 150, 155, 178, 184, 193-194
French Revolution 69, 193
Free enterprise 28, 130-131, 134-135
Fry, Stephen 80
Fund managers 13
Galax(y/ies) 52, 122, 189
Gates, Bill 80
Gaza 51, 150
Genetics 61, 177
Geocentric 69
Germany 155, 189
  German 162-163, 169, 179
Global(isation) 9-10, 20, 26, 33-35, 37, 40-41, 52-53, 56-57, 62, 65, 68, 73, 80-81, 89, 93-94, 98, 101, 103, 105-107, 111-112, 115, 128-129, 132-133, 144, 175, 176, 178, 183
  economic race 35, 73, 106
  economy. *See* Economy
  race 20, 35, 80-81, 94, 101, 105, 132
  village 35, 89
Gold(en/-) Standard 15, 115-118, 121, 123-126, 128-131, 169-170, 177-178, 184-186
Gollum 66
Government consultation 47
Greece 77, 112
  Greek(s) 67, 72, 87, 166, 181
  drama 87
Gross National Product (GDP) 36, 37, 191
Gulf States 36
Hardy, Oliver 139-140
Health(y/ier) 17, 35, 58-61, 93, 95, 97, 127, 143, 167, 183, 192
Hippocrates 59
Hiroshima 181
Hitler Youth 103
Hitler, Adolf 65, 103, 162-163
Holocaust 148

Homosexuality 49, 51
Housing 35
Huxley, Aldous 63, 80
International Monetary Fund (IMF) 37
India(n/s) 98, 118, 158, 166, 193
Industrial 21, 26, 30, 39, 70, 78, 83, 98, 100, 101, 111, 182
   Action 30
   Revolution 26, 30, 39
Infidels 65, 179
International affairs 50, 161
Internet 9, 22, 70
Iraq 147, 151, 153, 163, 181
Isil 103, 151, 153-154, 162-164
Islam(ic) 72, 99, 103, 111, 113, 144, 153-154, 156, 181, 194. *See also* Muslim
Israel(i/s) 65, 145-150, 153, 156, 166-167, 169,
Ital(y/ian) 38, 148, 163
Japan(ese) 100, 163, 179, 189
Jerusalem 145-146, 157, 167
Jew(s/ish) 51, 65, 72, 113, 144-145, 147-148, 156-157, 162, 172, 188
Joseph 174
Judaism 181
Justice 26, 49, 83, 87, 125, 161, 188, 189
   In- 16, 25, 47, 74, 84, 103, 105, 131, 143, 156, 164, 185
Karma 113, 119-121, 123, 138, 141, 143, 169
Keynes 115
Kurds 147
Labour (party) 94, 192
Large Hadron Collider 43, 127
Laurel, Stan 7, 139-140
LGBT 158
Little Red Book 103
Liverpool 98
London 98

LSD 48
Machiavelli 117
Mad Max 176-177
Mainstream medicine 59
Manipulations of the markets 23, 31
Mao. *See* Tse Tung, Mao
Marketing experts
Marx, Karl 83-84
Marx(ist/ism) 82-84, 162
Material resources 30
Media 9, 49, 62, 80, 82, 86-87, 89, 91-92, 137, 139
Medical 57-58, 69
Medieval
   Crusade(s/r) 147, 153, 157
   Europe 77
Meritocracy 78-79
Middle East 9, 46, 102, 144, 147, 148-151, 156-157, 163-164, 173, 194
   Mandate 147-151,
Monetaris(m/t) 35, 103, 133, 135
Mongol(s/ia) 77, 111
Moses 174
Muhammad 51
Multi-national companies 99
Muslim(s) 46, 103, 147, 153-154, 157, 162, 169, 172, 189. *See also* Islam
Mythology 65, 87
Nano
   technology 40
   vision 61
National Health Service (NHS) 93, 95
Nazi 163, 169
Nebuchadnezzar 110
Neo-colonial(ist) 10, 99, 175
New Deal 115
New York 36, 151-152,
New Zealand 166
Obama, Barack 151, 183

Index

Odysseus 67
Oedipus 67, 87, 116
Ottoman. *See* Empire
Pagan 65, 181
Palestin(e/ian/s) 51, 147-148, 150, 156-157, 166, 169, 187, 188
Persia 77, 110, 112
Pharaohs 110
Pharmaceutical 127
Pied Piper 147
Pizarro, Francisco 65
Planetary Cycles Mundane Astrology 178, 194
Pluto in Capricorn 14, 38-39, 69-70, 94-96, 132, 176-177, 185
Pol Pot 162
Politician(s) 11-13, 26, 36, 62-64, 69, 71, 79, 80, 91-94, 96, 133, 180, 187
Pope Francis, His Holiness 183
Post-
   colonial 35. *See also* Colonial
   truth 9-10
Premier League 44
Prince, The 117
Principled free-enterprise 114
Profit motivation 31
Profiteer(s) 26, 30, 135, 181
Prometheus 67
Promised land 147, 156, 174
Property investment 144
Protestant 77
Punk rockers 103
Qualitative research 64, 128, 130, 177
Quantitative Easing (QE) 38
Quantitative research 128
Ramadan 172
Rastafarian 46
Recession
   1930s 32
   1989-92 112
   2000 112

Reduction(ist/ism) 60-64, 67-68, 71-73, 114, 177, 192, 193
Reformation 68, 70, 130
Refugee 35, 85, 105, 157, 169-170
Regulator(s/y) 13, 92
Reign of Terror 184
Renaissance 62,
Roman(s)
   Empire. *See* Empire, Roman.
   Catholic Church 68, 69
   Church 112, 174
Rome 77, 110, 144
Romeo and Juliet 144
RT network 88
Rules of Acquisition 118, 193
Russia 40, 51, 83, 85, 88, 111, 166, 174
Satan 25
Saxe, John Godfrey 94
Schools' curricula 73
Scien(ce/tific) 5-7, 10, 26-27, 40, 56-67, 70, 72, 74, 83, 86-87, 92, 96, 117, 127-128, 130, 132, 135, 175, 177, 187, 189, 197-198
   method(ology) 60-62, 71-72
Secret Language of Astrology, The 53-54, 142, 191-192
Secular 62, 65, 71-73, 77, 128, 130
   Education 72
Sermon on the Mount 51
Sexual(ity) 49, 51, 63, 68, 103, 119, 142, 153, 158
   orientation 44, 46, 49, 192
Shakespeare, William 144, 193
Shambhala 118, 193
Sharapova, Maria 48
Sharia Law 103, 153
Shia 144, 147
Slave(s/ery) 56, 77, 85, 89, 115, 174, 182
   labour 30
Snow White 66
Social institutions 11

Social(ism/ist) 51, 83, 84, 189
Soho 46
South Africa 51, 164, 169, 193
South America 40, 98, 100, 187
South East Asia(n) 100, 105
South Sea Bubble 29
Soviet 22, 82-83, 166
Spain 103, 111, 157
Spanish 38
Speculative
 capitalist system 26, 114
 financial trading 101
 investment 29, 33
 profit and loss 33
Stalinist purges 184
Star Wars 66
Steroids 57
Sub-prime crisis 23
Sunni 144, 147
Sunyata 181
Sykes-Picot protocol 153
Syria 147, 153-154, 163, 166, 181
Tax havens 11
Test tube 11
Texan 46
Third World 100
Tibetan 118, 143
Titanic, the 111-112
Tobacco industry 127
Trade margins 30
Treaty of Versailles 163
Triple conjunction 132-133, 176
Trungpa, Chögyam 118, 193
Tsarist Russia
Tse Tung, Mao 104
TV soap characters 79
United Kingdom (UK) 49, 81, 93-95, 98, 171, 191-192
 government 49
United Nations (UN) 148

United States of America (US/USA) 24, 31-32, 36, 51, 85, 115, 148, 151, 156, 169, 170, 180
 economy 36
 Federal Reserve 22, 31-32
 southern states 51, 169
Univers(e/al) 23, 43-45, 51-52, 54, 57, 66, 69, 76, 122, 161, 182, 185, 188-189, 193
Universit(y/ies) 26, 73, 90, 104
Utopia 82-84, 184-185
Venture capitalists 14
Victorian 49, 158
Vietnam 103, 166, 181
Wall Street Crash 115-116
Warsaw ghetto 51
Washington Post, The 153, 194
Welfare 35, 81, 94, 131
West Bank 156, 167
Western economies 36, 100
Western exploitative capitalism 34, 100
Western world 100, 158
Wheel Turning Kings 76
Wikipedia 117, 193
Workers 13, 16, 30, 34, 63, 81, 83-84, 100, 105, 135, 144, 179
World Economy. *See* Economy
World free market economy 172
World Trade Organisation 34
World War One 56, 111, 153, 162-163
World War Two 94, 99, 103, 115, 146, 148, 163-165, 169, 179
World wealth 35
World Wide Web 27
X-ray 61
Yom Kippur 166
Yuppies 103
Zionists 156

Read the other three books in
Roy Gillett's *Astrological Quartet*

Beautifully designed full colour volume, to help you learn astrology from the beginning or be a companion to show friends and enhance your work.

Astrology & Compassion
the Convenient Truth

Roy Gillett

Know the real nature of astrology and its potential to benefit conventional academia and help clarify our legal, financial, social and learning problems.

Economy Ecology & Kindness

World Economy & Astro-cycles 1984-2024

What are the real causes and lasting solutions to our current crises?

by

Roy Gillett

To understand the fundamental systemic causes and real way to resolve the 2008 economic crisis.

Available at all shop and online outlets or email:
crucialbooks@virginmedia.com
http://crucialbooks.co.uk/